Robert Nicholas Barrett

In the Land of the Sunrise

A Story of a Japanese Family and the wonderful Land they live in

Robert Nicholas Barrett

In the Land of the Sunrise
A Story of a Japanese Family and the wonderful Land they live in

ISBN/EAN: 9783337170936

Printed in Europe, USA, Canada, Australia, Japan

Cover: Foto ©ninafisch / pixelio.de

More available books at **www.hansebooks.com**

IN THE LAND OF THE SUNRISE.

A STORY OF A JAPANESE FAMILY AND THE WONDERFUL LAND THEY LIVE IN.

BY ROBERT N. BARRETT, TH.D.

Author of "*THE CHILD OF THE GANGES.*"

LOUISVILLE, KY.:
BAPTIST BOOK CONCERN.
1895.

Copyright, 1895,
Baptist Book Concern, Louisville, Ky.

Electrotyped
BY ROBERT ROWELL,
LOUISVILLE, KY.

PRONUNCIATION.

ALL LETTERS SOUNDED.

a, as in father.
e-ei, as in prey.
i, as in machine.
o, as in bowl.
u, as *oo* in fool.
ai, as *i* in bite.
ch, as in chin.
g, as *ng* in finger
    (except at beginning).
h, fully aspirated as in he.
hi, almost like *sh*.

Japanese words have no variations for number and person.

TABLE OF CONTENTS.

Chap. I. Love's First View	11
Chap. II. The Miyai—They Meet	20
Chap. III. The Home-bringing	28
Chap. IV. The Lore of the Samurai	40
Chap. V. The Revolution	49
Chap. VI. Beginning of a New Era	56
Chap. VII. In Kioto	62
Chap. VIII. On the Tokaido	72
Chap. IX. Life in Yokohama	82
Chap. X. A Pilgrimage to Nikko	93
Chap. XI. Among the Ainu	108
Chap. XII. A Painful Discovery	117
Chap. XIII. Christ in the Family	127
Chap. XIV. Life in the Capital	133
Chap. XV. Elevating the Masses	142
Chap. XVI. Off for Harvard	149
Chap. XVII. After Four Years	155
Chap. XVIII. A New Movement of the Young People	163
Chap. XIX. The Light Grows Brighter	169
Chap. XX. Outlook Before the War	173
Chap. XXI. Conflict and Victory	180
Appendix. Literature on Japan	190

LIST OF ILLUSTRATIONS.

Dedication	3
A River Scene	13
In Bed	20
Tea Girl	27
Mr. Kimura's Garden	36
Hara-Kiri	56
Carrying Baby	57
Shitenoji Temple and Pagoda	63
Mikado's Palace and Gardens	65
The Great Bell	69
Dai Butsu	78
Yokohama and Harbor	80
Art Gallery	83
Street in Yokohama	84
Basket Maker on Way to Market	86
Bridge in Kioto	70
Halting for Refreshments	76
Mt. Fuji	77
Sacred Bridge	94
Approach to the Temple, Nikko	97
Yomeimon Gateway	100
Nearer View of Yomeimon	101
Golden Shrine of Iyeyasu	103
Tomb of Iyeyasu	105
Ainu Men	112
At Dinner	129
A Modern Improvement	134
Kiku (Chrysanthemum)	157
Girl and Samisen	163
Priest and Assistant	165
Y. M. C. A. Hall	176
Sayonara	189

PREFACE.

THE AUTHOR does not hope to add any new information on the subject of Japan, nor is the present volume intended for critics and scholars, but for thousands of our people who really know very little of the country and its people. I have simply designed to give to such a pleasant introduction to one of the most remarkable, as well as one of the most important nations in the world, and then refer them to books better suited to a critical study.

Among the many books written about Japan a few are by thoughtful men and women, and are the results of mature study and sensible observation. Others are but the ephemeral ravings of pleasure-seekers who look upon the Japanese as a nation of artistic clowns, whose sole destiny in the world is to furnish amusement for the thousands of "globe-trotters" who annually pass through their flowery land. It never occurs to the latter that these have souls to be saved or lost, and they regret to see the breaking up of the old fascinating immorality, much of which can not even be referred to in print.

Even among the best books it is almost impossible to obtain one of convenient size, and at reasonable cost, that gives anything like a rounded conception of the country and the people as a whole. Most all deal with special topics; some discuss the Geography, others the History, or the Women, Children, &c. Hence, in order to get a just conception, you must read several books on different features. The present volume is designed to fill that want. It looks at the country and the people from every standpoint, and in an impartial spirit. It avoids the extremes of those who, on the one hand, despise Christianity as a factor in shaping the nation's progress; and that of others who are zealous for religion, but fail to give the people themselves due credit. We should be fair to both sides. Japan is the strategic point of the Orient. Through her we are to develop and evangelize China, Corea and Tibet. Thus "Japan and the Japanese" well deserve our attention.

The book is written in the form of a story, true to life, and dealing with the subject in a way not hitherto attempted. The Author is grateful to learn that his former book has been instrumental in leading some to give their lives to the evangelization of the world, and it is his prayerful hope that the present little volume may inspire some to labor for those interesting people whom he has learned to love, both from association and from history.

THE AUTHOR.

Louisville, Ky., June 1, 1895.

INTRODUCTION.

LAND OF THE SUNRISE! Land of the lotus and cherry blossoms; of towering mountains and reedy plains; of peaceful rivulets and foaming torrents; land of curtain-concealed Mikados and warlike shoguns; who has words to describe its unique characteristics, or the wisdom to glean from the wealth of its mythology the golden threads of its history!

The archipelago of Japan lies off the eastern coast of Asia, and stretches from the extreme north to the Philippine Islands on the south. The Chinese knew of no land beyond it, and spoke of it as the "Land of the Sun's Origin." The first knowledge we have of the country is from Marco Polo, a famous Venetian traveler who sojourned for several years at the court of Kublai Khan in China during the thirteenth century. He called it *"Chipangu* (Sun's Origin)," and described it as follows:

"It is an island towards the east in the high seas 1500 miles from the continent; and a very great island it is. The people are white, civilized and well favored. They are idolators and are dependent on nobody. And I tell you the quantity of gold they have is endless, for they find it in their own islands."

From the Chinese word, *"Chipangu,"* the Japanese formed the word, *Nippon*, (Sun's Origin), and prefixed the word *Dai* (Great), making *Dai Nippon*, by which name they designate their wonderful land.

Christopher Columbus read what Marco Polo said of these remarkable islands, and set out to find them, going westward, since the maps of that day showed no lands lying between them and Europe. The result was the discovery of America.

The climate and productions are greatly varied, both on account of its physical features and its position. If placed in the same relation to America as it sustains to Asia, Japan would reach from Massachusetts to northern Florida. It has the appearance of a sunken mountain chain whose innumerable peaks come through the surface of the water and form its groups of islands. The shores are bold and precipitous like mountain walls, and gashed with narrow green dells, picturesque and beautiful.

The main island has no name, but is usually called Hondo (Main Island). North of it lies Yezo, or Hokkaido, and to its south are Kiushiu and Shikoku. The aggregate area is about equal to that of California, and the population is 40,072,000. The principal cities are Tokio, Kioto, and Osaka. It is at the latter place that our story begins.

IN THE LAND OF THE SUNRISE.

CHAPTER I.

LOVE'S FIRST VIEW.

IT WAS a soft dreamy night in Osaka, the great commercial metropolis, called by some the "Chicago" of Japan. The stir of business had ceased in the great gloomy factories, the shops were open, and the streets and water-ways were gayly lighted with thousands of many-colored paper lanterns. The ugly merchant junks that had plowed the canals all day were now motionless, tied to their moorings, and the way was left clear for the hundreds of pleasure-boats that began to throng the water. So many of the broad streets have stone-walled canals through the center, the "highways" for so much traffic, that Osaka has been likened to Venice; but a glance at the quaint architecture on each side destroys the comparison. Hundreds of high arched bridges span the canals at intervals. They were evidently constructed with a view to the convenience of boats passing under, and not for vehicles passing over, for at this time they had no vehicles.

On a bridge overlooking a popular resort stood two young men of the *samurai* class looking down upon the fairy scene below. Many house-boats were occupied by whole families, who took advantage of this opportunity to refresh themselves after the heat of the day, so intense in the low shimmering plain on which Osaka is situated. Very conspicuous were the gaudily decked thatched boats of the *geisha* (singing girls), who sang like sirens in the twilight and drew crowds of infatuated beholders to flock like moths around their alluring lanterns and sit under the spell of their *samisens* (guitars). One of the young men, Matsuda Kimura,* whose father was one of the most trusted retainers of the lordly *daimyo*, who dwelt in the frowning castle beyond the moat, suddenly dropped the conversation in which he had been engaged with the young man at his side, and began gazing with unfeigned admiration upon one of the gay floats. His cousin, Okubo Sakamune, watched him with interest. The boat was an unusually large one, and seemed to be occupied by a wealthy family. The father and mother were watching the antics of a chubby baby boy as he rolled upon the mat clutching at an orange that persisted in rolling just beyond his reach. But that was not what interested Matsuda; for at the other end was a group of young girls just budding into womanhood, engaged in some kind of a frolicsome play. They were prettily dressed, as Japanese girls usually are, their embroidered silken *kimonos* (outer garments), held in place by broad belts tied in enormous bows behind, looking especially charming under the light of the festoons of many-colored lanterns

---

*The Japanese, when at home, place their family name before the "given" name, as Kimura Matsuda, but for convenience I write it as they do in this country.

above and around them. Three of the girls, who seemed to be visitors, were inclined to be lively, and when the old folks were not looking were rash enough to shake their long sleeves by way of flirtation with some boys in a neighboring boat—a great impropriety in Japan. The prettiest of all, and by far the

River Scene.

most charming, evidently a daughter of the elderly couple, refrained from such mischief, though she was not lacking in merriment, for that is a characteristic of young life in Japan. She it was who had unconsciously attracted the attention of the young *samurai* on the bridge.

"I beg pardon, honored cousin," finally broke in Okubo, "but what is it that attracts you?"

Matsuda started and blushed, as he caught himself in what he feared his cousin would think a very foolish act. His first impulse was to evade the truth and say that he was admiring the reflection of the stars in the water, but he was a true knight, and frankly replied,

"I crave your pardon for my rudeness, but I confess I was so attracted by that face yonder in the boat that I forgot myself. It is very foolish in me, I know, but I was bewitched before I knew it."

"I do not consider you foolish by any means," answered Okubo, who was already married. "All Japanese love beauty, whether in nature or art. You were not flirting, and there is nothing wrong in admiring the beauty of that young lady, who is indeed unusually charming. I have often wondered whether you were susceptible to such impressions, and if you ever thought about your marriage which is shortly to take place. Your parents are getting old now, and must soon turn their estate over to you. As it was I who acted as go-between several years ago in securing your betrothal to Miss Toki Morita, the daughter of your father's friend, it is but natural that I should be interested in what concerns the happiness of both of you."

Here they were interrupted by the passing of a procession, and were forced to move on with the crowd, going in the direction of Matsuda's home.

"Will you graciously condescend to enter?" he asked, as they stood before the door.

"You do me great honor," answered Okubo, bowing low. "I shall be glad to see the honorable father."

"I think you will find him at the fountain in the garden," said Matsuda. "I will remove my swords and join you in a few minutes."

"Thanks," replied Okubo. "I know his retreat, and shall easily find him."

With these words he passed through the sliding walls of the little parlor and into the exquisite little garden, a necessary and luxurious part of every Japanese home. Numerous paper lanterns suspended from the most favorable positions increased the enchantment of the natural loveliness, though the rising moon was now peering over the eastern wall. It was a lovely spot of ground, and Mr. Sakamune did not wonder that the old gentleman delighted to spend his quiet evenings there. Though but a tiny spot, as all Japanese gardens are, it had been so carefully cultivated for many generations that it was a perfect landscape in miniature. In it were trees a hundred years old that you could almost put in your pocket, some of them trained into the shapes of all kinds of animals. A stream of clear water leaping over the wall dashed down two or three miniature precipices, formed a miniature lake, then branched out in trickling rills among the flower-beds, passed under miniature bridges, around miniature islets, and then disappeared at the other side. Mr. Sakamune passed along the well-kept gravel walk and by the little lake sparkling with gold-fish gentle enough to eat from the hand. Lotuses floated on its bosom, and irises and azelias fringed its borders. From here a path with a border of ever glorious national chrysanthemums led to the cascade beyond. Here, sitting under the overhanging boughs of a weeping willow that grew out of the wall and drooped its branches in the dancing water, swaying up and down in time to the musical ripple of the stream, was Mr. Kimura. He was a pleasant old gentleman of the polite ceremonial type now fast dying out under the encroachments of Western worldliness. He arose at once, and with genuine pleasure visible on his refined features, exclaimed,

"Ah, it is my honored nephew, Okubo Sakamune! Graciously be seated on my humble mat, I pray you?"

"You are too kind to one so unworthy," replied Okubo. "Your seat is a luxury."

With that they both sat down by the water side, and Sakamune began at once to tell the object of his visit.

"I am happy to announce," he said, "that I have been very successful in the task you assigned me. Unsuspected by himself I led Matsuda to a position where I could study the effect of female attractions upon him. I am sure he will be happy when married, and I would lose no time in making the arrangements. I even mentioned the matter to him, but the crowd prevented his replying. I have no doubt that he is thinking seriously about the matter."

"You have done well," replied the old gentleman, "and I thank you for the satisfaction you have brought me. I must soon retire from active life, and it is necessary that my son should be installed in my position as early as possible. While it is not customary nor necessary to consult the wishes of the young people in such matters, I am anxious that my home shall remain one of peace, and, in order that such may be the case, it will be well for them to see each other once, and see if their own judgments ratify the action of their parents. It was for the purpose of ascertaining whether Matsuda had any thoughts aside from military matters that I requested you to lead him unconsciously among the attractions of society. It now remains for Matsuda and Toki to meet each other. I leave the matter with you. Hark! he is coming. You may meet him and consult with him about the *miyai* (look-at-each-other meeting). Whatever he says you may do. *Sayonara* (Good-bye)."

Mr. Sakamune then departed, and meeting Matsuda by the little lake, joined arms with him, and as they proceeded back toward the house, he said:

"Honorable cousin, your father wishes your marriage with Miss Morita to be consummated as soon as possible, and he also graciously allows you and the young lady to meet according to the prescribed rules of etiquette, so that you may mutually judge of each other. I am therefore authorized to propose to you three kinds of meeting, either one of which you may select. We will meet her on the bridge as she walks with the *Okkasan* (mother), where you may observe her as she approaches from the other side; or we will call upon her at her home, where you may receive a cup of tea from her hand; or, finally, we will occupy a box near her at the theater, where you can study her and enjoy the delectation of feasting your eyes upon her for a whole evening.* What is your excellent choice? It shall be done."

Most young men would have preferred the latter, but Matsuda was wise beyond his years. His ideal of a wife was not a woman whose chief accomplishment lay in posing on a bridge or simpering in a theater. A corrupt *geisha* could do both to perfection. He wanted a home-maker, and so he replied, to the surprise of Okubo:

"By your pleasure, I prefer to see the young lady at home. I can best judge of her there."

"Very well," answered Okubo. "It shall be as you wish."

"There again comes up the vision from the bridge," said Matsuda. "It is wrong for one so soon to be married to admire so much the beauty of a stranger. I almost wish I had not seen her. If I only knew that my betrothed looked anything like her I should be satisfied."

"Then let me put your fears to rest," answered Okubo, "for Miss Morita is, in my judgment, fully as pretty as the girl you saw to-night. But it is now near the hour of the ox (midnight), so I must be going. I will call for you to-morrow. *Sayonara.*"

---

*The Japanese take lunch to the theater and stay there all day.

It is difficult for an American or European young man to conceive the anxieties that beset Matsuda at this point. Although he had been prepared to assume his father's swords and his position as retainer to the *daimyo* (prince), he was now being thrust into a position in regard to which he had given little thought. Since his admiration for female loveliness had first been awakened that night at the bridge, he naturally wondered if his betrothed would be pretty. That is, in Japanese conception, if she would be graceful and slender, with small hands and feet, pearly teeth, and rosebud mouth. But he checked himself. His father had decided, and that must suffice. Although, according to Japanese custom, he had never met his betrothed, he had often heard his father speak of Mr. Morita as a wealthy merchant who had been able to purchase the rank of a *samurai*. He must be an unusually excellent character if such a man as Mr. Kimura could so far overcome caste prejudice as to seek the hand of his daughter for Matsuda. No doubt she was an estimable young lady. So Matsuda resolved to try to be satisfied. A wise conclusion, for he was unable to help himself if he had not been satisfied. To marry against the will of the parents was an unheard-of thing.

CHAPTER II.

THE MIYAI—THEY MEET.

THE NEXT MORNING there was no small stir in Mr. Morita's house. Toki had been informed that she was to meet her betrothed that afternoon, so special preparations had to be made. Her hair had been dressed only two days before, but this morning

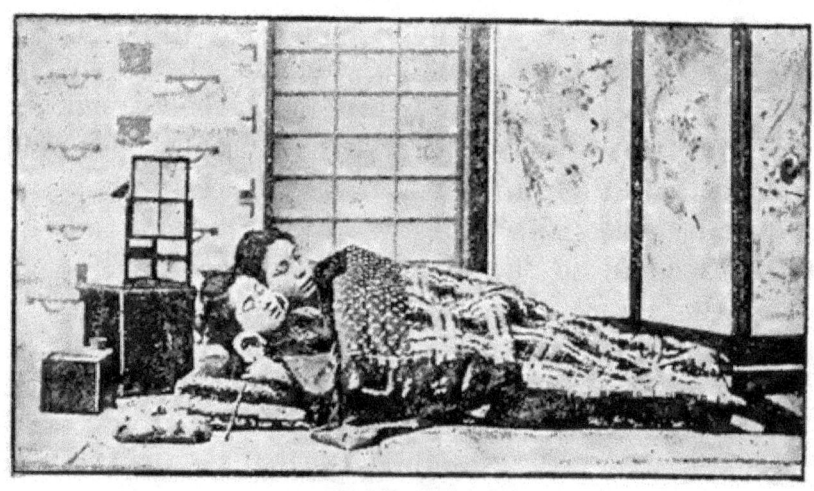

In Bed.

the modest little hair-dresser was surprised to receive a summons to come and do her work a day earlier than she was due, for fashion in Japan decrees that the hair shall be arranged in such ornate style as no woman can do for herself, and so the professional hair-dresser is called in two or three times a week. Of course, to sleep on a pillow would necessitate this being done every day, which would be both inconvenient and expensive. For that reason pillows are not used, but blocks of wood, with cotton pads on top, supply their places and support the back of the head.

Little Miss Snow, who had dressed Toki's hair for several years, and who is now an intimate friend, came with all speed and began her work with a skill born of long practice. But the motions of her deft fingers did not prevent her feminine tongue from wagging incessantly. She was cunning, and playful, but sympathetic.

"I beg many pardons, gracious lady," she began, "but it is something strange for me to be here to-day when I should have come to-morrow. Now something is going to happen. I knew that some one would be seeking the hand of the rich merchant's daughter. I doubt not many have already been refused. Pray who is the fortunate one?"

"Thanks for your compliments, Miss Snow," replied Toki, "but have you not heard that I was long since betrothed to Matsuda Kimura? He comes to-day, and I must meet him."

"What, the gallant young *samurai* who lives near the castle, whose father is a relative of the great *shogun!*"

"He is the very same," replied Toki with a little blush of pride. "What do you know of him, Miss Snow? I have heard much about the patriotism of the family, and their standing socially, but how are they at home? Does not your friend dress Mrs. Kimura's hair? Are they kind to each other and to the servants? And Mrs. Kimura, will she treat me as a human? Oh, I have heard so much about the harshness of mothers-in-law! Tell me if you know anything of them at home."

"What a frightened little dove it is!" said Miss Snow, twitting her playfully. Then, becoming more serious, she answered:

"Allow me to congratulate you on the fact that you are about to enter one of the best families in Osaka. The old people are highly cultured and very kind. There is only the one son, and I have no doubt that you will be treated as kindly as in your own home. Besides you have had greater advantages than most of the young wives who come to grief, in that you have had such an excellent mother to train you and fit you for your station, so that your mother-in-law will find but little, if anything, to complain of. It is true, Matsuda has given little attention to anything except martial exercise, but I know him to be chivalrous and brave, and that means that he will not neglect you.

"By the way, if Matsuda had been on the canal last night wouldn't he have been jealous, though! I saw some mischievous young men making signs towards your boat, and, though I could not tell who it was that answered, I caught the glimpse of a pretty sleeve dangling coquettishly over the railing."

THE MIYAI—THEY MEET.

"O, alas!" cried Toki, blushing furiously. "Is it possible that you could think of accusing me of such a thing! So much for companions. There were some thoughtless girls on board who did such, and now I must bear the blame!" She was about to burst into tears when Miss Snow answered reassuringly:

"There, there, pretty one! No one accused you. I knew who did it, and just wanted to tease you. I beg a thousand pardons in that I have unintentionally distressed you. There, now; why, you were about to spoil your rosebuds (lips). My tongue is always running away with me. Any way, you looked unusually pretty last night, and I could not have blamed the boys if they had so far forgotten themselves as to flirt with you, though you did not with them."

At last the shapely head was properly adorned, and after a few more pleasant little courtesies and good wishes for the future, Miss Snow bowed herself out and left Toki for her maids to dress in a style befitting the occasion.

Promptly at the hour appointed Mr. Sakamune and his young hopeful dropped their clogs* on Mr. Morita's front porch and were ushered in by the bright-eyed little servant girl. She led them past the kitchen—always in front in a Japanese house—back to the charming parlor, which opened out upon a lovely little garden in the rear, if possible more lovely than the one at Mr. Kimura's. Then she placed a soft mat for each to sit on and in a few moments brought

---
*The Japanese wear heavy wooden clogs for shoes, and, of course, these could not be worn in the house, as they would ruin the delicate mats on the floor. For that reason they are always left on the outside.

in tea in tiny cups, a cup for each, on a little lacquer table not more than four inches high. She then bowed herself out and went to announce their arrival to Mr. Morita.

In due time that much dreaded, but kindly polite old gentleman appeared, bowing very low, and sucking in his breath audibly as a sign of respect to his guests. Matsuda found it very natural to draw in his breath just then, for never in his life had he had an experience that he so much dreaded. He would rather meet a hundred armed soldiers than one prospective polite old father-in-law. But Mr. Morita was very gentle, if he was dignified. He said by way of welcome,

"How can you, honorable sirs, condescend to enter my humble home?"

"Nay," they replied, "you do us great honor to allow us to sit in your august presence. Pray be seated."

After numerous bows and compliments on both sides they finally sat down. It was the custom on such occasions to be very formal, and in conversation to avoid all reference to the matter in which all were most interested. So Mr. Morita began,

"You young *samurai* hear much of what is going on, what is the latest news from the American ships?"

Mr. Sakamune replied: "A special dispatch from Yedo by way of Kioto announces that the shogun has made a treaty with Perry, and that trade is to begin between the two countries at once. An American

Minister is to be located at Yokohama, which is to be an open port."

At this Mr. Morita seemed to be much excited. "And what do you think will be the result of such an action?" addressing Matsuda, who had not spoken. He ventured to reply timidly,

"I think it will be the greatest blessing that could happen to Japan. Our country being opened, we shall stand side by side with the other great nations of the world; for that they are great is easily seen from the great ships and the models of other wonderful things that they bring. I think Commodore Perry is a benefactor."

"I totally disagree with you," said Mr. Morita. And grasping the hilt of his sword he exclaimed, "I would behead every one of the upstart barbarians. What right had they to interfere with us. Being a merchant, I am, of course, interested in traffic, but I want no traffic with those uncouth hairy creatures. Why, I hear that they eat swine and frogs, and drink a fiery liquor till their faces become red like fire, and that they know nothing of our etiquette. They can not be a high type of humanity. It is a shame that the god-given Land of the Rising Sun is to be polluted by their unhallowed feet."

Needless to say this speech was not very encouraging to Matsuda, and he did not venture to reply. But Mr. Morita's politeness asserted itself and he immediately apologized,

"I beg your lofty pardon for becoming so excited, but I really do abhor these foreigners. As a man, however, you have an equal right to your opinion, and I should not have spoken so abruptly." So much like a born *samurai* did he appear that it was hard to realize that he had always followed the peaceable pursuit of a merchant.

At this point the host observed that the cups were empty, and he clapped his hands together sharply as a signal to bring some more tea. Now did Matsuda's heart beat wildly, for he knew that the arrangement was for his betrothed to bring the second cups. It was with difficulty that he appeared to join in the stilted conversation which the other two gentlemen kept up for the next few minutes.

At last the gilded screens were pulled aside and Toki entered. Matsuda could scarcely restrain an exclamation of surprised delight, for there, in even greater loveliness, stood the girl he had fallen in love with the night before. One glance sufficed to impress his mind with her face, and another her dress. Her long flowing garments, held in place by the richly embroidered *obi* (girdle) were becomingly beautiful. She wore no jewelry, save an ornament in her hair. Her face was fair to look upon, oval in shape, with carmine tinted lips, damask cheeks, and large gentle eyes with long drooping lashes.

She advanced in a slow and dignified manner, and with downcast face as etiquette demanded. But in spite of her outward calmness her whole being thrilled as she knelt and placed the cup before her betrothed and lifted her eyes to his face. One look passed between them, a low salute, and she was gone, having been less than one minute in the room.

Whatever he may have dreaded before, Matsuda could have no further apprehension now. So he sincerely answered, "I will," when Mr. Morita suddenly dropped the discussion of foreign invasion and asked him if he would take her.

Tea Girl.

They now joined in a cup of tea and then walked across to the Government office, where Mr. Morita had Toki's name transferred from his own family register to that of Mr. Kimura. Legally speaking, she and Matsuda were now married. There only remained the formal home-bringing.

CHAPTER III.

THE HOME-BRINGING.

SOME little difficulty was encountered in fixing upon an early date for the marriage ceremony, the Japanese having so many unlucky days upon which it would be disastrous to marry. Finally a day was set, and both families began their preparations. According to the usual custom, the ceremony was to take place at night at the home of the groom's father. During the preparation Toki received many handsome presents, which she displayed at home for a few days, then sent on to be arranged in the room which she was to occupy as a bride.

Mrs. Morita had faithfully instructed her daughter from childhood as to her duties in the home, but now she saw fit to add to the preparation of her wardrobe some hints as to how to perform her duties as a wife. So one day as they were sewing on the delicate fabrics the mother said:

"You remember, my daughter, how I have tried to instruct you in womanly ways, and I am happy to say that you have conducted yourself fully in accordance with my teachings so far—but you are now about to experience a great change in your life. You will be no longer subject to a loving father and tender mother, who, for the affection they bear you, can overlook little faults; but you are going to live with comparative strangers, and serve a man whom you have never seen but once. While I know the family to be kind and generous, still your happiness and my honor will depend largely upon your conduct as a wife.

"Much is said about the cruelties of mothers-in-law, and I know that they do often abuse helpless young wives; yet many girls enter upon married life with scarcely any conception of their duties as wives and daughters, but care only for frivolities, so that it is no wonder that nervous old women lose patience with them. By following my directions you will have no trouble, I am sure, with either your husband or mother-in-law. Have you in reach the book I gave you on your last birth-day, *Onna Daigaku* (*The Greater Learning for Women*)?"

"Yes, honored mother. Shall I get it?"

"Bring it to me, please."

Toki opened an elegant little lacquer toilet stand and took from it a neatly covered book which she handed to her mother, who said:

"Now in this book, which contains the wisdom of the great moralist, Kaibara, you will find laid down everything pertaining to your duties as wife and mother. Have you read it entirely through?"

"Yes, indeed; more than once."

"That is good Still there are some specific rules that I wish you to memorize, and I shall write them down here in the back."

After she had finished writing she said:

"You see there are thirteen of these, and I will

read them to you, so that they may become my last words of instruction."

"'1. After marriage you are legally my daughter no longer. Yield to your father-in-law and mother-in-law the same perfect obedience that you have yielded to your father and mother.

"'2. Your husband is your only lord and master. Be humble and polite. Perfect obedience to the husband is a noble trait in a woman.

"'3. Be kind always to your mother-in-law.

"'4. Do not be jealous; that is not the way to win your husband's affections.

"'5. Even when there is injustice on your husband's part, do not be angry, but be patient, and when he is quiet reason with him.

"'6. Talk but little. Do not tell another's mischief. Never tell a lie.

"'7. Get up early, stay up late at night, and do not take a nap in the day. Do not drink much wine, and do not go into a crowded place till you are fifty years old.

"'8. Do not ask a fortune-teller what your future destiny will be.

"'9. Though you are married young, do not associate with young men, even if they be relatives.

"'11. Do not wear gay dresses. Be clean always.

"'12. Do not be proud of your father's prosperity or position, and do not boast of them before your husband's family.

"'13. Always be careful how you treat the man-servant and the maid-servant.*'"

"I thank you greatly," said Toki when her mother had finished, "I am sure these will be of great service to me, and I shall not forget them. Now please to advise me about some less important things, but

---

*For a fuller quotation, see "The Japanese Bride," by N. Tamura.

things I do not fully understand. How about blacking my teeth and extracting my eye-brows after I am married?"

"Well, as you know, custom requires such of every married woman to distinguish her from the unmarried. So after you get into your new home that will be one of your first duties. I will give you a pair of tweezers, and your maid can assist you about your eye-brows. True, it will be somewhat painful, but by pulling them out by degrees you can endure it."

"Ugh! What a horrid practice, anyhow," said Toki with a little shudder. "Why is it required? It makes beautiful girls hideous old women."

'I am sure that I can not tell why it is done," answered her mother. "There are contradictory accounts as to its origin. Some say that women formerly did it to render themselves more attractive in the eyes of their husbands. Others say that the husbands required it in order to render them so unattractive to other men that they would not have other admirers than their own husbands, and so there would be no cause for jealousy. At any rate, a woman so distinguished is as safe from the approaches of other men than her own husband as if she were surrounded by a Chinese wall."

"I should think so," said Toki. "How could they be admired?"

"Do not forget, my daughter, that your own mother has passed through that 'hideous' change. It is our lot and we must submit to it. There should be some distinction between married women and those who are not. That is the main reason also why you must leave off your gay dresses and your red undergarment, for such are the distinctive apparel of virgins alone. You are not undergoing anything worse than I have already endured, and I am sure I did it gladly for my husband's sake."

"Pray excuse me, honorable mother. I never thought of you when I spoke so rashly. It never occurred to me that you were not good looking, and it seems perfectly natural to see you as you are, for I never saw you before the change. If you look so well now you must have been beautiful then. Anyway, I shall not complain again." Here Mrs. Morita was called away and the conversation dropped.

At last the eventful day arrived. Toki arose early and pushed away the *shoji* (blinds) breathlessly to see whether the weather was propitious, for to get married on a rainy day would be a very unlucky thing—to the new dresses at least. But the morning was clear and bright, so she set about her preparations with a light heart. After her bath, which every Japanese takes as regularly as the daily meals, she submitted herself again to Miss Snow, who was to dress her hair for the last time.

"Ah," said the active little hair-dresser, "so I am to lose a good customer, for you are no more to have your hair arranged in the style of maidenhood. Tomorrow you will wear it 'high,' like a matron. Well, it is a great honor to be married, especially to such a man as Matsuda, and I congratulate you. Still I regret to see you pass out of my bounds. May Lord

Buddha give you peace and a long life." Thus she rattled on till her task was accomplished and she had to leave in order to give the bride time to dress and make all her preparations before Mr. Sakamune should call to conduct her to her husband's home.

It was late in the afternoon when Toki came forth ready to go, for marriages are always at night. She looked very pretty in her wedding dress of pure white silk folded over the breast, its long flowing sleeves almost touching the floor. Her *obi*, the most important and most extensive part of her outfit, was a girdle of gold-embroidered velvet wrapped twice about the waist and tied in an enormous bow behind. Her tiny feet were encased in white silk moccasins, with separate divisions for the great toe, or "foot-thumb."*

A little after nightfall Mr. Sakamune and a few friends appeared, followed by a *norimono* (palanquin) borne on the shoulders of four men. Then came the most trying time for Toki. She was placed inside the *norimono* and borne away like a corpse, while funeral fires were kindled before the doors, thus signifying that henceforth she was dead to the old home. Mr. Sakamune, clad in stiff ceremonial robes, led the procession, followed by the parents of the bride, the special friends, and servants bearing rich presents for the family and servants of the groom. As both parties were in high social standing it was observed that many lanterns were hung along the street just

---

*Japanese clogs are held in place by straps passing between the toes and around the ankle. Hence the division.

without the doors of friends who thus offered their congratulations.

Mr. Kimura's house and garden were brilliantly lighted, and the best room was gorgeously decorated for the occasion. New mats were laid on the floors, clean white paper was pasted on the frames of the sliding doors, and blossoms of pine or bamboo in rare old vases adorned the *tokonoma*, the raised floor of one end where the ceremony was to take place. In the middle of the floor stood a little table on which was a pine tree, emblem of unfading youth, and sitting at each end of which were two large dolls dressed as an old man and an old woman, signifying long life to the young couple.

When the *norimono* arrived at the gate Mr. Sakamune assisted the bride to alight upon the clean white mat that had been spread from the door, and turned her over to the charge of her two maids, who had gone on before to arrange her room and who were to assist her in perfecting her toilet. She was ushered to her room, and in a little while was made ready. A little touch here, smoothing out a wrinkle there, a little more carmine on the lips; then she drew on the thick silken vail and proceeded to the room where the company was in waiting.

A large company of relatives and friends was present, all silent and solemn as the grave. Matsuda was already seated on the *tokonoma*. With beating heart, but steady, dignified step, Toki approached and took her seat beside, but a little below him. Mr. Sakamune, who as go-between was to officiate in the ceremony, took his seat in front of the couple. Then two voices in an adjoining room began to chant a low sweet melody which continued till the ceremony was over. A little table, on which was a pagoda-shaped pile of three tiny cups, was handed to the bride. Then two little girls came forward with the ceremonial *sake* (rice wine) in two bottles decorated with male and female paper butterflies. Each poured the sake from her bottle at the same time into a pretty little copper kettle, thus symbolizing the union of the two lives. Then one took the kettle and filled the top cup on the table in the bride's hand. She took three sips and passed to Matsuda, who drained the cup and placed it under the bottom of the stack. The next cup was filled and disposed of in the same manner, and so with the third, making for each nine sips in all. Then Toki lifted her vail and looked blushingly into the face of her husband, as Mr. Sakamune now pronounced Matsuda to be.*

The bride and groom now retired to their respective dressing-rooms to change their stiff ceremonial robes for something more comfortable, and more in keeping with the festivities soon to begin. The guests in the meanwhile dispersed to the garden and wandered around admiring its lakes, fountains and flowers.

At last husband and wife reappeared, and all were invited into the dining-room. What a scene awaited them! Artists and cooks had conspired to reproduce

---

*Many a man never saw his bride till she herself raised the vail after the "nine sips."

Mr. Kimura's Garden.

the loveliest parts of Dai Nippon's glorious landscape in a form that could be enjoyed by other senses as well as that of sight. There were fruits piled into snow-crested Fuji, hills and promontories, inlaid with streams of jelly and lakes of delicious liquids of various kinds. The choicest vegetables were modeled into trees and flowers.* It seemed a pity to destroy such a picture, but after a spirited attack of chopsticks wielded by deft fingers the smiling landscape became a desolate waste as if smitten by typhoon or earthquake.

The feast lasted nearly three hours, during which time the bride, according to custom, changed her dress three or four times. What a chance to show all her pretty clothes! All the friends exchanged cups of *sake* with the couple, and, to see them drinking with each of their friends, you would think that they were sure to become intoxicated, especially after the "nine sips." But the drinking was mostly a matter of form, and they really drank very little. You should remember that the cups were only a little larger than thimbles, even if they had been filled each time.

Just before midnight the guests began to disperse, but so polite were they that no one spoke of "going home," which would have been a sad reminder to the bride who had just died to home. But all left with pleasant words of parting or a thrust of humor. No one kissed the bride. No, indeed! they had never

---

* The Buddhist religion forbids the eating of flesh, though a distinction is made in regard to fish. Sometimes a deer is eaten, conscience being stifled by calling it a "mountain whale."

heard of such a practice, and there was not even a word for kiss in their language.

Mr. Sakamune had done his part well in bringing the matters to a final issue, and he had been engaged at it for several years. Matsuda and his father appreciated his services and rewarded him with a handsome present.

* * * * * *

Toki dressed early next morning, and tripping to the room of her new parents before they arose, bowed her pretty head to the matted floor and inquired if they had slept well, and how they felt. She then proceeded to the kitchen according to the suggestion of her mother and made herself acquainted with the servants, and prepared with her own hands the tea for breakfast. She was determined that no fault should be found with her in the matter of industry. She soon won the esteem and affections of the servants so that she never afterwards had any trouble with them.

The consideration with which children are taught to treat servants accounts, no doubt, to a large extent, for the fact that there is no servant problem in Japan Servants rather take a delight in doing the best for their employers, even surprising them frequently with what they accomplish out of so little material.

After a few days Toki was allowed to visit her former home and remain with her mother for a week. This is the time when many young brides refuse to go back to their husbands, and the go-between has to secure a divorce. But Toki seemed perfectly happy, and no such thoughts entered her mind. After a few days Matsuda joined her, bringing presents for her family as she had carried to his. Mr. Morita provided a rich feast and invited his friends to come and meet his son-in-law. The two then returned home, and after Toki had gone with Mrs. Kimura to call on all who had placed lanterns in front of their doors on the wedding night, they settled down to quiet home life. Toki assisted her mother-in-law about the house-keeping, knitting, sewing and embroidery; while Matsuda busied himself in practicing the arts of a *samurai*, such as horsemanship and sword exercise.

CHAPTER IV.

MATSUDA LEARNS THE LORE OF THE SAMURAI.

AFTER MATSUDA returned with Toki from her father's house, Mr. Kimura decided that it was now time to install him in the position of *samurai*, and as proprietor of the home; for in Japan young people never go into houses to themselves, but live with the parents of the groom, and perpetuate the family line from the old home. As they were talking on the subject in the garden next morning, Matsuda said:

"I shall be only too happy, most honored father, to do what I can to extend the glory of our house, and I am profoundly sorry that you feel the necessity of giving up active life before I am old enough, or have had experience enough to understand my duties better. I should like to have some information from yourself as to the past, so that I may know how to act in the future. Of course, I know the nursery tales, but I want to learn the real history of what pertains to the *samurai*. Our mission is both political and religious, and as we have two religions and two rulers, I am somewhat at a loss. In the first place, please to explain Shinto as it relates to the government of the country."

"I gladly comply with your request, my son, as far as I am able," replied Mr. Kimura, "especially since it is such an important question."

"Shinto, as you know, is simply devotion to the Mikado as a divine being. Our tradition teaches that Japan is the direct creation of the gods, and that the Mikado is the son of a goddess.

"Izanagi and Izanami, male and female divinities, stood together on the bridge of heaven, having received commission to produce the 'Land-of-Reed-Plains,' and as they looked down into the abyss below, Izanagi dipped his jewelled spear into the ocean and stirred the briny deep. When he drew it forth brine dripped from its glittering point and formed the four thousand islands on which we live. They then descended and made their abode on the land with the intention of creating other worlds. But fair Izanami died and went to Hades. Undaunted by the terrors that opposed him, Izanagi plunged into the depths to bring her out, but he was driven back covered with pollution. When he washed his august person many deities were formed, the Sun Goddess springing from his left eye. He was so pleased with her shining face that he gave her dominion over the day to give light to the islands.

"But on a certain day the Sun Goddess became offended with her brother and hid herself in a cavern. Then were the islands dark. In vain did the other deities beseech her to show her face again. They finally hit upon a happy thought. A great metal mirror was made and set before the cave. They then began to shout and seemed to be in great glee. When the Sun Goddess inquired the cause of their sudden joy, they told her that they had found another goddess more beautiful than herself, and that they were praising her. The Sun Goddess, jealous at the thought of a rival, came forth to see if what they said was true. When she saw the reflection of her own shining face in the mirror she thought it really was another goddess, and was so astonished that she did not notice when the entrance to the cavern was closed behind her. Then was the 'Land-of-Reed-Plains' light again. That, my son, is the origin of the metal mirror, and explains why it is found in all Shinto temples.

"Now our first Mikado was the eldest son of the Sun Goddess. His heavenly name being too sacred to repeat, he is known to us by his posthumous title, Jimmu Tenno. By the authority of his divine mother he descended from heaven in a gilded boat, and with a host of mighty warriors drove out the Ainos, the hairy aborigines, and took possession of the land. Since then his direct descendants have ruled down to the present day. That, in brief, is the origin of the Mikado and the Shinto faith."

"Now I understand," answered Matsuda, "why it is that the Mikado is called divine. But another difficulty arises; if he is so highly honored, how is it that we have another ruler of such power as the shogun?"

"That," replied Mr. Kimura, "grows out of the reverence of the Mikado of which I was speaking. Since he is worshiped as a god the Mikado can not appear in public as a man, which would degrade his person, but must remain enshrined in his temple like palaces at Kioto, while the actual administration of the government is placed in the hands of another less sacred person. The secular affairs of the government were originally administered by powerful lords whose families were related to the Mikado. About six hundred years ago these princes fought among themselves for the supremacy, so that the country was thrown into a bloody civil war. Yoritomo, head of the great Minamoto family, by the authority of the Mikado, conquered the warring factions and placed himself at the head of affairs. For his bravery the Mikado rewarded him with the title of '*Sei-i-tai-shogun* (Barbarian-subjugating General),' the highest title that any subject can receive. Yoritomo won his success mostly through his brave and faithful brother, Yoshitsune, who really led the armies, but his very success led Yoritomo to envy him and to drive him from the country lest he should use the power he had gained to exalt himself. Some say that Yoshitsune went to Yezo and lived among the Ainos, teaching them useful arts; others that he escaped to China, where he became the great ruler, Kublai Khan. But you have heard from infancy the stories about Yoshitsune.

"Yoritomo established himself at Kamakura, but afterwards removed to Yedo*, where he built the great castle that became the center of a vast city. Here he was virtually autocrat of civil affairs, though nominally receiving orders from the Mikado at Kioto. Everybody obeyed the shogun, but feared and reverenced the Mikado."

---
*Now called Tokio.

"Thanks, honored father," said Matsuda, "your explanation removes my difficulty in that matter, but I pray you have patience with my stupidity a little further, and tell me one more thing. Why is Japan cut off from the great world of which the Dutch traders tell us; and what is the meaning of these terrible warnings written on signs at every crossing? They condemn foreigners, and call them *Kirishitans* (Christians). Who are they, and what has religion to do with the banishment of foreigners?"

"An answer to that," replied Mr. Kamura, "involves the whole story of our national religions, as well as politics. As related, Shinto is the national religion, but about twelve hundred years ago Buddhism was introduced. Shinto has no forms of service and no creed, except devotion to the Mikado, hence it was not hard for the two religions to become fused. Under the shoguns Buddhism has gained great headway and somewhat overshadowed the national religion, though not supplanting it. Between two hundred and three hundred years ago a new religion appeared which has caused all our trouble. A young man convicted of a crime in Japan, fled to India, and there met a missionary priest named Francis Xavier, leader of a Kirishitan sect called Romanists. The young man united with them and led Xavier to Japan.

"The Romanists made their religion very popular with its gorgeous ritual, and its concessions to existing forms. They did not demand much change on the part of the native priests. Temples were called churches; Buddhist priests were called Christian priests, and performed their functions very much as formerly; images of Buddha, by a few touches of a chisel, became Yasu (Jesus), and the Goddess of Mercy in like manner was transformed into Mary, the mother of the barbarian God. Converts multiplied so rapidly that in little more than a generation they numbered 600,000, including many of the *daimyo* themselves. Presents were sent to Rome, and allegience was acknowledged to the Pontiff. At one time the great city Nagasaki was entirely Christian.

"But the priests of the rival orders, called Franciscans and Jesuits, quarreled among themselves, and said so many hard things about each other that the people lost confidence in the priesthood. About this time Hideyoshi, the shogun, heard of a conversation that fanned the smouldering fires of discontent into a flame of fury. Some one asked a Portuguese ship officer, who was a Romanist, how it was that his King had gained possession of such a great part of the world. The man unwisely replied,

" 'The King, my master, begins by sending priests, who win the people, and when this is done he dispatches his troops to join the native Christians, and the conquest is easy and complete.'

"No wonder Hideyoshi was enraged and alarmed. He immediately issued an edict expelling all foreign religious teachers from the land. Several priests of both orders were even burnt alive in order to enforce the command.

"At the death of Hideyoshi the shogunate passed

into the hands of the present dynasty, under Tokugawa Iyeyasu, Japan's greatest statesman. Iyeyasu decided that the suppression of the wicked foreign religion was necessary to the safety of the empire, so he banished both native and foreign adherents. They were exported by shiploads, and thousands were massacred in the most horrible manner. Although it was a corrupt and dangerous sect, still it seems that their humanity should have preserved them from the mutilations that followed; for some were torn asunder by oxen; some were tied up in rice-bags, thrown into heaps and burned alive; others were tortured by spikes driven under their nails; and still others were starved in cages with food placed in sight, but just without their reach. But enough of such things. You will read of them in the books. In spite of these severe measures it was impossible to persuade the poor deluded souls to deny their wicked creed, though they really knew very little of it. They had only been taught a few prayers in some kind of a barbarian jargon, something like '*Pater Noster*,' '*Ave Maria*,' or other such things as none of them understood. Yet they willingly died for their faith. Then the signs to which you refer were placed at the crossings condemning to certain death any Christian, or even the Christian's god, if he ever set foot on the shores of everlasting great Japan.

"This answers your other question, as to why we are secluded from the world. Iyeyasu thought he could best develop the people if they were cut off from all foreign interference, and so for more than two centuries no foreigner has been allowed to approach our shores, with the exception of the Dutch traders, who have been restricted to a single island. Nor has any Japanese been allowed to leave.

"You may not know that Iyeyasu was the founder of the great feudal system as we have it now. He let out provinces to great lords, or *daimyo*, simply requiring of them military support. The retainers of the *daimyo* who fought the battles of the country were the *samurai*, the next highest in rank. From us have come the scholars and the men of culture. Beneath us are the merchants, artisans, farmers and other laboring men. Still, a merchant, by means of his wealth and character, may become a *samurai*, and thus be on social equality with us. That is why it was possible for me to marry you to the daughter of a former merchant."

"Now," said Matsuda, "that brings us to the question raised by my father-in-law the first time I saw him, 'What do you think of the shogun's policy in treating with the foreigner now at Yokohama, and what will be the result?' I, perhaps rashly, answered that I thought it a great thing for the country; that we had been secluded long enough, and now, if these countries are so great as they seem to be, we may come into contact with people equally as civilized as ourselves, if not more so, and that we may derive great benefit from them. But Mr. Morita almost frightened me by exclaiming that he would like to behead every one of the foreigners, and clutching his sword as if he were going to begin at once. Is that a general feeling, and do you think trouble is likely to follow?"

"I fear that my friend's patriotism exceeds his judgment," replied Mr. Kimura. "There may be some difficulty, and there are many who are fanatically opposed to such a movement; yet, without doubt, it will be for the advancement of our country. I should be glad to see the shogun's action ratified, not simply because I am myself of the Tokugawa family, but because I love Dai Nippon, and am anxious to do all I can for her advancement. It may become your duty to fight for this, and so I would encourage you to keep yourself in good practice for warfare. It is now your hour for exercise, so we will not talk further to-day."

CHAPTER V.

THE REVOLUTION.

ONLY a few days after the scene of the last chapter it was found that the muttering storm had broken forth. A fleet runner, naked save a breechcloth, rushed into the castle at Osaka bearing a government dispatch in the split end of a long stick, summoning the *daimyo* and his retainers to hasten to Yedo, the shogun's Capital. Matsuda, having taken his father's place as *samurai*, was enlisted, and buckling on his two swords he mounted his warcharger and rode away. Although Toki little understood the cause of such a sudden summons she was brave and patriotic, so that she gave him up without a word. That evening, sitting by the *hibachi* (firebox), she asked her mother-in-law what the trouble was.

"I see, my dear," said the old lady kindly, "that you have been so engaged in your preparations for marriage that you have not paid attention to current events. You have done right, for hitherto such things have not concerned you; but now, as the wife of a soldier, you should be instructed in all that pertains to his life, so I shall gladly relate the circumstances of the present trouble as best I am able."

"Thanks,' replied Toki, "I shall be greatly interested in what you have to say."

"Well, you know, of course, that for more than two hundred years the great Tokugawa dynasty has ruled in Yedo, and that within that time no foreign barbarian has been allowed to place his foot on our shores. During all these years the Mikados, worshiped as gods, have remained enshrined in their ancient gardens, giving themselves to religious exercise, never speaking to the public except once a year, when the shogun bows in the solemn stillness without and listens to the proclamation of the august will spoken in sepulchral tones from behind the sombre curtains. The Tokugawas, from whom your husband is a descendant, are related to the royal family, and hence have had almost unlimited power. But there are other mighty princes who think that they have an equal right to power, and who are using every pretext to seek the overthrow of the shogunate. Although that has never yet been attempted, yet what they think a sufficient pretext has at last happened. About a year ago great ships came to our shores from a land far beyond the seas. They were commanded by a man named Perry, who brought a letter from his ruler, the President of the United States of America, asking our 'Emperor' to make a treaty with him for the purpose of trade, and that his ships might land here on their way to China so that they might renew their supplies, since it is a long voyage. Having delivered the letter to the shogun, whom he thought to be the sole ruler, he departed, saying that he would return after a year for an answer.

"At first all the princes objected, since they thought these 'hairy barbarians' unworthy to associate with the offspring of the gods. But when Perry returned recently, bringing many marvelous things which he said were made in America, some began to think that after all they might be equal in intelligence to us. He has cars that run on iron rails without any horses to draw them. Also he put up wires, and two men at either end several miles apart communicated with each other. Many other such things he has shown, so that many have come to the conclusion that it would be a wise thing to sign the treaties and open trade with such a wonderful country. During the year the shogun has died and been succeeded by a mere boy, who has been controlled by the princes who are in favor of opening the country. Instigated by them, he has signed the treaties without saying anything to the Mikado, and even keeping for himself the letters and presents sent to the 'Emperor,' so that the Americans think he is really the sole ruler. Of course, he will secure the ratification of the Mikado, who would not have conferred with the foreigners anyhow, and he will doubtless deliver the letter and the presents when the time comes for him to go to Kioto for instructions. But he signed the treaties under the title of '*Tai-kun*,' a Chinese word for 'Great Ruler.' This incensed the opposing princes and caused them to rebel against the shogun. Everywhere they are raising the war-cry: 'Expel the barbarians and honor the Mikado!' Hundreds of fanatics have deserted their daimyo and become *ronin* (outlaws), wandering at large over the country and cutting down with their sharp swords all who oppose them. It is not so much zeal for the Mikado nor opposition to foreigners, as it is a blood-thirsty desire to overthrow the shogun, who really is not responsible for what he has been forced to do. That is why the *daimyo* and his forces must hasten to the Capital, for the country would be filled with blood if these outlaws should accomplish their desires. To-morrow you and I will go to the temple and pray great Lord Buddha to give success to our troops, and to protect my son and your husband."

"I am very grateful to you, honored mother," said Toki when Mrs. Kimura had finished, "and I do humbly hope that the trouble will soon be over."

But these fond hopes were not soon to be realized. It seemed impossible to stay the great uprising. The popular ambition seemed to be to drive back every foreigner from the shore. But the foreigner continued to come in increasing numbers. Seventeen other nations soon secured treaties, ports were opened, Ministers were established, and the great ships continued to plow around in the adjacent waters to protect those on shore. It was plain that the foreigner was there to stay. Vengeance must be had on the shogun. He had secured the ratification of the Mikado to his treaties, but only his blood could satisfy the thoroughly enraged opposing princes. He was forced into battle—an unheard-of thing for a shogun and his people—and after three months of desperate fighting he fled to the stronghold at Osaka, where he died in great distress at his downfall.

The Tokugawa princes now selected a new shogun, Keike, whose sole qualification consisted in his weakness, and his pliancy in the hands of his masters. But they overreached themselves. If he was afraid of his friends he was equally, if not more, afraid of his enemies, so when the latter advised him to resign the shogunate to the Mikado and retire, he did so at once.

Just previous to this the Mikado, Komei, a bitter opposer of the foreigners, had died, and had been succeeded by his son, Mutsu-hito, the present ruler, and the one hundred and twenty-first in his line. The new Mikado readily accepted the resignation of the shogun, and thus, on the 30th of January, 1868, he brought to an end the double administration, himself becoming the sole and active ruler.

But Keike had only "jumped from the frying-pan into the fire." He had appeased his enemies, but had mortally offended his friends. They immediately influenced him to change again and take up arms in the effort to reinstate himself in the shogunate. But in this rebellion against the "Son of Heaven" he lost irretrievably the respect of his vassals. It was plain that the *prestige* of the shogun was at an end. Failing in battle he fled with his retainers to the stronghold of Osaka, closely pursued by the loyal troops, who burned the citadel, as they thought, over his head. But he made good his escape through the assistance of Mr. Kimura. The old man, now in his dotage, deeply chagrined at the downfall of the Tokugawa house, and vaguely hoping that the shogun might yet be restored, had gathered a few strong men, and himself covered Keike's retreat, fighting desperately with the overpowering forces. He was captured just before the burning walls fell in, but by this time the ex-shogun was in a fishing craft far out on the bay. The old *samurai* was imprisoned as a traitor against the Mikado, but Keike, from a safe hiding place, sent his apologies to the Capital, begged the royal pardon, and promised never again to take up arms against the government. His request was generously granted, and he retired into private life at Kamakura.

The young Mikado felt the thrill of life in his veins. Shaking off the vail of obscurity that had been around the throne for more than two thousand years, he looked boldly out over his dominions and observed the real condition of his people with a sympathetic interest that no Mikado had ever exhibited before. Disregarding the superstitious traditions as to his sanctity, he thought himself none too sacred to look after the interest of his subjects. He soon pacified the outlawed fanatics who were causing so much trouble, and who, after the defeat of the shogun, the more readily yielded to the foreign policy of the Mikado.

It now appeared that there were many wise scholars who had secretly learned foreign arts and sciences from the Dutch, and who had been using their influence in arousing a disposition among the people to shake off their sleep and to welcome the western world in its desires to benefit them. These were now appointed to learn all they could from whatever sources, and to disseminate useful information among the masses of the people.

About a week after the Restoration the young Mikado horrified the conservative elements of his empire by announcing that hereafter he would assume personal control of the government, and that he was going to give a public reception to the foreign ambassadors, whom he would meet in person. This announcement created the wildest excitement. The Son of Heaven has never been allowed to show his face even to his own people, and shall he show himself to the barbarians! Desperate efforts were made to prevent the meeting, but it took place according to arrangement. The people began to see that their ruler had both common sense and power, and they respected him. He discarded the idea of divinity as only a cunning stroke of policy by mediaeval despots who desired to gain the abject obedience and fear of their subjects. He simply wished to be a man among men, and to lead his people to a higher life.

CHAPTER VI.

BEGINNING OF A NEW ERA.

AFTER fourteen years of bloodshed and confusion we return to Osaka to find our family much changed. Mr. Kimura had been confined in the castle, condemned to death. Had his case been laid before the Mikado as was that of the ex-shogun, he, too, might have been pardoned, but as it was he was subject to the circumstances of war. Being a man of high estate, and of hitherto unblemished character, he was allowed the privilege of *hara-kiri** in order that he might wipe out from his family name the stigma of his guilt. So, in the presence of his intimate friends and relatives, who sincerely applauded his action, he knelt upon a thick mat placed to receive his blood, and cheerfully plunged

Hara-kiri.

---

*This was suicide by ripping open the bowels with a sword. To a Japanese this was the quickest way out of misery. When men are surrounded in battle they account it ample revenge upon their enemies if they can succeed in taking their own life. A criminal, by committing hara kiri atones for all his crimes and dies with an untarnished name. The most ignominious punishment is to deny a man this sacred privilege.

the sharp sword into his abdomen, dying within a few minutes, and leaving behind him a name as honorable as that of any loyal soldier who had never taken up arms against the "Son of Heaven." All his property, as well as his official authority, now became Matsuda's.

By this time Toki's heart had been made happy by the arrival of three children, two boys and a girl. The eldest son, as is often the case, was named Ichiro (First Man). Then came the bright-eyed little girl whom they called Kiku (Chrysanthemum), after the national flower. Saburo (Third Man) was the youngest, and as round and jolly as the most of little Japanese boys are.

By the time little Chrysanthemum was four years old a large doll was tied to her back and she had to carry it there all day, whether she was eating, playing or running errands. She soon learned to balance it there, and became accustomed to it so that it neither annoyed her by its weight nor was in any danger from falling by her stooping too far.

"What a strange idea!" you exclaim

Not at all. Nearly all little girls carry dolls, and they do it as near like their mothers carry babies as they can, but Kiku was being trained for a special purpose. When she was six years old her last brother, Shiro, was born, and when he was only a few weeks old he was placed on her back instead of the

Carrying Baby.

doll. Kiku had herself been carried in that way by the little maid-servant, and now she must perform the same service for the baby brother. Little Shiro seemed perfectly at home; his smoothly-shaved head, with only a ridiculous tuft of hair left on top and at the sides, bobbing from side to side, or lying fast asleep on Kiku's shoulder, while she ran about seemingly perfectly unconscious that he was there. Almost any day in the streets of a Japanese city you may see many little girls carrying on their backs fat little chunks of rosy-cheeked humanity almost as large as themselves. In many cases where there is no elder sister, nor maid-servant, the mother carries the child herself, and does all her work with the little one on her back instead of crawling on the floor and crying after her.

Matsuda's father now being dead, his mother came entirely under his own care and control. She now called nothing her own, though both Matsuda and Toki showed her the same respect and affection that they had before. She remembered though that it is the place of a widow to be under the control of her eldest son, so she took her place as one of Matsuda's children, and Toki became sole mistress of the household.

* * * * * *

We now come to the most remarkable event in the political history of Japan—an event such as never occurred in the world before—the termination of feudalism by the voluntary petition of the feudal lords themselves. The feudal system was distinctively a part of the Shogun's government, having been founded by Yoritomo and perfected by Iyeyasu. Since the shogunate had been abolished it seemed fitting to the *daimyo* that they should surrender their territories to the Mikado and become his subjects in the same way that other citizens were, provided that they receive sufficient means in return to pay off their standing army, the *samurai*. Accordingly, on August 7th, 1869, at their own request, the Mikado decreed that the *daimyo* should surrender their estates to the throne, abandon their titles and become citizens of honor.

Japan now encountered a problem that no other nation probably has ever confronted. The aristocratic *daimyo*, numbering 268 families, had voluntarily resigned all their rights and their property, a thing unprecedented in history. Under them were the *samurai*, numbering 400,000 families, "the backbone of the land," whose sole living was by the sword. But swords are now to be beaten into plow-shares, and what are they to do?

For awhile the *daimyo* were made governors over their respective districts under the appointment of the Mikado, and only gradually removed as other positions opened up for which they were fitted. The government itself undertook to settle with the *samurai*, who were now left penniless. It borrowed $165,-000,000 and paid them off in round sums of money. But the *samurai* had always lived from hand to mouth, and did not know how to take care of money, so that in a little while many of them were in as bad state as ever. They had been taught to despise labor, since they were a grade higher than the laboring classes. So many of them found it hard to make a living. The only thing was to become scholars, which many of them did, some attending the great American and English universities for that purpose. Matsuda, however, was wise enough to save his portion, and manage to live on it until something should open up for him to do.

With the dispossession of the aristocracy came the elevation of the lower classes. There were the *heimin*, farmers, merchants, artisans, etc.; the *hinin*, the "not-human," and the *eta*, the outcasts, who handled dead carcasses, skins and other such things as would defile a Buddhist. Fully 32,000,000 of these lower classes had never been recognized as the citizens of the country. They were now given legal standing along with the higher classes, and thus Japan approached nearer a "government of the people, for the people, and by the people." All classes are now on an equal footing as far as legal standing is concerned.

The Emperor* having now become the real ruler, it seemed best for him to quit his mysterious seclusion and take up his abode in one of the other great cities; some recommended Osaka. He considered the matter and decided to occupy the castle of the shoguns at Yedo, which now became Tokio (Eastern Capital). He thus centralized about himself all the outward signs of power which his position demanded.

---
*The word Mikado is now discarded.

BEGINNING OF A NEW ERA.

The Emperor realized the advantages to be gained from western education, and this led him to employ teachers from both America and Europe to come and teach for a few years till an educational system could be established. The ambitious and high-spirited sons of the *daimyo* and *samurai*, being now without employment, turned their attention to higher education, both as a means of culture and as a qualification for service in the government, which now demanded capable officers. So a large number of the brightest of the land have attended Oxford, Yale, Harvard, and other great institutions.

Matsuda took special lessons from an English teacher at Osaka, so that he could take care of himself in the new order of affairs. He, like his father, had supported the Tokugawa house in opening the country, and took great interest in the improvements that were being made. In the year 1872 the first railroad was opened up between Yokohama and Tokio, thereby greatly increasing the commerce between the two cities. Through the influence of a friend, Matsuda received appointment to a position as revenue officer at Yokohama. So, having disposed of his home at Osaka, he shipped his goods by sea to Yokohama, and prepared to go through by land with his family, as it was now in the fall, the pleasantest part of the year for traveling. The women and children had never seen the country, and his mother wished to visit some of the temples and shrines on the way.

CHAPTER VII.

IN KIOTO.

KIOTO was a day's journey from Osaka and on the road to Yokohama. The railroad had not yet been constructed between the two capitals, so the usual mode of travel was by boat. Matsuda hired one of the long flat "gondolas" that make frequent trips up and down the river, and prepared for the journey, which he decided to make by night in order to avoid the heat of the sun. The boat had a long, low cabin in the center, about four feet high, on which the passengers could sit as long as they wished, and in which they could retire to sleep when the air became too damp to sit without.

Osaka was in her evening glory as the boat passed from the quay by the light of the rising moon. Thousands of people had congregated on the banks of the water ways, on the picturesquely curved bridges, and on the hundreds of gayly decked little houseboats that thronged the water. Some of these were inhabited by families who could be seen taking their ease as they sipped their tea. Others were crowded with merry young people who made the air ring with peals of laughter or strains of music from the *geisha's samisen*. On every boat were several paper lanterns shedding their mild crimson glow over the quiet family circle, while the pleasure crafts were brilliant with strings of light streaming from the most gayly colored lamps. The boys on the shore delighted themselves with shooting off fire-works, which circled with graceful coruscations over the water, adding to the brilliancy of the scene. Here and there were boats loaded with fruits and confections making their way among the other vessels and offering their tempting stores for sale. It was a beautiful sight,

Shitenoji Temple and Pagoda, Osaka.

and one that impressed itself on the memory of those who were departing, as they glided silently along the still water of the canal, between the stone walls on either side, and beneath the high arched bridges that spanned the water in great numbers.

On reaching the main stream the boat shot forward rapidly as it was propelled by eight half-naked coolies who ran back and forth from bow to stern with long poles thrust in the sand of the bottom of the river. Almost all night they kept up their regular march with marvelous endurance. They kept up a guttural noise all the time, enabling them to keep step, since there were four on one side and four on the other side of the cabin By morning the passengers awoke and looked out to find that they had reached the shallow sand-bars near Kioto, and that the coolies were out on the bank with a long rope with which they were pulling the boat as they ran along through the tall grass of the river's border. At Fushimi, a suburb of Kioto, they landed and proceeded by *jinrikishas** (native carriages) to the main part of the city, arriving by the time the sun was up.

Since the death of her husband grandmother Kimura had become "*Go-inkio-sama*," that is, she had retired to that state of elderly life, the "Beulah" of a Japanese woman's pilgrimage. Then women give up all interest in active life and spend the remainder of their days in devotion at the temples and shrines, doing no work at home, but being waited upon by all the household. It is the only period of real rest and pleasure in the life of many women. The poor down-trodden wife or sadly mistreated daughter-in-law is enabled to bear up under the burdens of life in anticipation of the time when she shall become "*Go-inkio-sama*," and be treated with honor and respect. It is, alas, the only taste of heaven that many poor souls ever have.

---
*Pronounced jin-reé-ki-sha.

Matsuda kindly volunteered to remain for a few days at Kioto, the city of temples, and the center of religion and refinement for all the empire. This would give his mother time to visit the most noted temples before they should settle down at the great commercial foreign metropolis at Yokohama, where she would no more have such an opportunity. Being well acquainted with the city himself he conducted

Mikado's Palace and Gardens.

her from place to place with true filial devotion. Of course, they went first to the palace and viewed the sacred precincts where the Mikados had lived entombed for seventeen centuries.

In keeping with the superstition that he had descended from the Sun Goddess, the Mikado was required to dwell in a house resembling a temple. No other houses in the empire, except Shinto temples, were allowed to have roofs shaped like those on the buildings of the Mikado's palace, with their peculiar curves resembling the sagging top of an oblong tent. Each room is a separate building with its own individual curved roof, and united to the next by its covered veranda. There being many rooms, the whole resembles a great collection of tent-shaped buildings, said to be a relic of nomad life when the tribes used to pitch their tents together around a common center, or court, in the highlands of Asia, whence they really came, instead of from heaven. Also, in keeping with the bare forms of Shinto, no paint or color is allowed to be used on the buildings, but the wood is of the finest grain and is kept smoothly polished. Sometimes the dark ends of the rafters are tipped with white, thus giving a pretty checkered effect to the somber eaves.

Around the palace is a large garden, cool, shaded, and secluded from outward view. Around the inner enclosure of the palace grounds is a yellow wall, marked all around with five white stripes denoting imperial possessions. Outside of this wall is a larger enclosure containing the palaces of the court nobles. Around the whole are a strong wall and a deep moat, thus forming a little imperial city cut off to itself apart from the other buildings of the capital.

The Emperor had already departed in his gilded closed *norimono* to Tokio, so that the place was not altogether as awe-inspiring as formerly. Heretofore the divine rulers had been surrounded with the most mysterious silence. When it was necessary for his Highness to utter his proclamations he sat behind a thick screen and delivered his mandates in a deep muffled tone that thrilled with awe the prostrate hearer on the floor without. No wonder his every command was obeyed, for all thought that he had the authority of a god. That is all there is in Shinto; no worship of images or of heavenly beings, no moral code, no creed; only devout reverence for, and obedience to the Mikado. Shinto had fallen largely into disuse during the last few centuries on account of the exaltation of Buddhism by the shoguns. But since the Restoration of the Mikado Buddhism had been disestablished, and Shinto again became the national religion.

Aside from its palaces, there is much in Kioto to fill a visitor with rapture. The situation of the city is one of the most delightful in the whole of this most beautiful country. It stands embowered among trees on a broad plain like a great floor, surrounded with a wall of evergreen hills and purple tinted mountains. On one side, at some distance, is the blue lake Biwa. Around and through it flow sparkling rivers with branches led through channels cut in the streets, giving to the place an aspect of delicious coolness and quietude. The straight streets are perfectly parallel, and cross each other at right angles. They are very broad and exquisitely clean. The small low houses situated in such spacious squares would look monotonous, but that is happily avoided by the luxuriant gardens and ancient groves, with a limitless variety of temples and pagodas. The hillsides blossom with gardens.

The greatest scholars and artists collected at Kioto. Here were manufactured the finest articles of porcelain and other wares for the two courts. This is also the home of silk industries. The court dress consisted almost entirely of silk, wool not being used. Almost every home has its silkworms, whose product supplies the living of thousands of people. In the year 1887 there were 16,864 bales, of $133\frac{1}{3}$ lbs. each, shipped to the United States alone.

All these things are interesting to sight-seers, but pious old grandmother Kimura was absorbed in visiting as many as possible of the thousands of temples that thronged the hillsides, peeping out from their solemn groves of ancient cryptomeria, or towering over their perfectly kept gardens, in some of which are wonderful little trees grown into the shapes of ships in full sail, or of animals and birds of various kinds. One of the first temples that she visited was that of "The Thirty Thousand Gods." It was a building 400 feet long, in the midst of which stood an image of the Goddess of Mercy, Kwannon, having ten faces, and 1,000 hands with which to dispense her benefits. On each side of her are 500 other images standing in ten rows to a side, making 1,000, each of which is five feet high and gilded. Each of these has ten smaller images on its head and ten in each hand, making 30,000 in all.

On her way home every evening she always visited the great bell that hung in a temple near their lodging. This bell is one of the most remarkable illustrations of the Golden Days of Buddhism under the shoguns. It is nearly fourteen feet in height and nine feet in diameter, weighing more than sixty-three tons. It is immovable, as all Japanese bells are, and is struck by a beam suspended from the roof, pulled back and forth by a rope. No words can express the thrilling melody of the deep tones that roll forth from its great bronze mouth in soft undulations that are yet so strong as to cause the very earth to vibrate in unison. When it sounds the whole community is still, rather feeling, than listening to the harmonious cadences that rise and fall on the evening breeze, tingling every nerve of its 300,000 listeners. No wonder an ancient religion associated with such sounds is so hard to overthrow.

The Great Bell.

Every evening the family went, with thousands of others, to the river flats, where there was always a cool breeze at night. This river, like most others in Japan, was a broad torrent in the rainy season, but in dry weather it was only a silver streamlet trickling over its sparkling shingle bed from side to side, forming many islets that seemed to be made for the purpose of furnishing sites for the most unimaginable fairy scenes. Here were thousands of lights from swinging paper lanterns, and thousands of merry people thronged the shores and islands, clad in their most bewitching costumes of silk with embroidered girdles. Quaint little bridges led to the diminutive

Bridge in Kioto.

islands which were covered with stands for fruit or confections. On some there were illuminated stands for tea, which was served by pretty girls, whose very looks and manners rendered sugar unnecessary and unthought of. At least you would suppose so, for sugar is never used. Platforms extended out over the water with surrounding railings for protection. On the floor of one might be seen a group of old men smoking their little pipes, three whiffs at a time, and discussing the affairs of the day. On another, near by, was a group of women sewing and chatting. A chubby baby rolled on the floor struggling to reach a gayly colored fire-fly, and a row of brightly dressed lasses leaned over the railing, laughing and talking, admiring their reflections in the water below, and slyly shaking their sleeves at the boys who were watching them from the other side. In spite of all their rigid etiquette girls will flirt, and though not allowed to speak to the objects of their admiration, the language of the fan and the waving sleeve is as intelligible and impressive as that of the lips.

It is sad to think that all this happy looking scene must soon vanish like a gay bubble, and that the people must perish with it. No happy life beyond for them; no hope, except for eternal forgetfulness. Well may they enjoy their little day while it lasts.

CHAPTER VIII.

ON THE TOKAIDO.

THE Tokaido is the great thoroughfare, or "Eastern Sea" road, running between the two capitals. It is 307 miles long, and was built by the shoguns to furnish safe and rapid transit from their seat at Yedo to the Mikado's throne at Kioto. No visit to Japan is complete without a ride on the Tokaido. Matsuda procured five *jin-riki sha* runners, and on a cool morning started early for his distant field of labor.

The *jin-riki-sha*, or "man-power-carriage," is a large baby-buggy on two wheels, drawn by a naked cooly instead of a horse. They are very light and make surprising speed. A trained runner will trot along at the rate of six miles an hour for forty miles at a stretch, only halting occasionally for refreshments while passing a tea-house, when he renews his tattered straw sandals and mops the perspiration from his tattooed body, smiling blandly all the time. But is it not an expensive mode of travel? Six cents per hour. So, with a fast runner, you get your ride for one cent per mile.

It was a delightful experience to the children, as well as to the women, to travel for the first time on the national highway. From infancy they had known the names of the fifty-three stations by heart. One of the favorite games of Japan is a game of cards played for a goal, which is a coin or piece of cake placed at the end of fifty-three spaces and called Kioto, each game won being a station reached on the way. In this way they had learned them so that they could repeat them in order from either end. Now, as

Jin-riki-sha.

(Runner covered with a rain-coat.)

they sat in their queer little carriages, they found much amusement watching the two-legged pony trotting along with his curiously pictured back glistening in the sun, and clapping their hands with delight as they passed one after another of the old familiar landmarks which they recognized, though they had never seen them.

All varieties of the life of populous Japan are represented on the Tokaido, though one can get a full conception of the poverty of the lower classes only by leaving the beaten track and going through the interior. All along the road on each side could be seen the rice paddies, with the light wooden houses in the midst, some distance from the road. Many villages thronged the road, and the runners had to be careful to keep from running over the children that were playing in the middle of the streets. There were no horses used on Japanese streets then, so that children were allowed to make their play houses there with perfect security that they should not be trampled upon. Tea-houses with their ever-present smiling girls were abundant. There was no thought of privacy anywhere, since, as we have seen, the rear of the house, which we would conceal, is always toward the street. Mothers could be seen dipping their dimpled offspring into the bath tubs sitting on the veranda. Public bath rooms were open to full view, men and women going in and coming out indiscriminately, with no thought of there being any impropriety in so doing. In the village a woman sat in her tub two feet from where the *jin-riki-sha* passed, calmly scrubbing herself with a bag of rice bran, seemingly unconscious that there was any one near, at least perfectly indifferent to the fact. Passers-by were equally indifferent, for they noticed her no more than they would a hog lying in the sunshine.

On each side of the road was a row of tall cryptomeria, or ancient pine trees, meeting overhead and

ON THE TOKAIDO.

forming a dense shade that had blessed many generations of tired and thankful pilgrims. Streams also frequently ran along by the roots of the trees, adding to the refreshing influence of the checkered shadows of mid-day when the sun was beaming down on the glistening fields without. The road was hard and smooth, and the *jinrikisha* sped along at a lively rate. The party frequently stopped for a day at a time at some of the most interesting places on the road, there being no special need for rushing. A Japanese never hurries, unless it is a cooly who is paid to do so.

Before crossing the Hakone hills, *jinrikisha* had to be exchanged for *kago*, basket-like contrivances suspended on poles carried on the shoulders of two men. Here they were carried over a steep rocky foot-path, sometimes meeting rows of pack-horses in single file led by men in blue blouses and head-dress of blue-and-white towels, the ever-present garb of the peasantry. Sometimes they would meet a woman clothed only in blue cotton trousers and leading a little pack-horse heavily burdened. From the Hakone range there is a magnificent sight of glorious Fuji-yama, the Hermon of Japan. It seems to rise up boldly from a plain, lifting with symmetrical curves its snow-crested summit to the clouds that love to linger upon its sacred peak. It is a beautiful sight to see its glistening head, on a quiet Summer's day, towering 12,000 feet above the plain, and surrounded with a filmy white cloud like a halo, intensifying the deep blue of the sky above it. But there is no more sublime and magnificent sight than the sleeping beauty when it is enshrouded by dark storm-clouds, and swept by tempestuous winds. The Japanese have a legend that Fuji arose from the earth in one night, leaving, far away near Kioto, a corresponding depression which formed the clear blue Lake Biwa. It is a holy mountain, and contains many

Halting for Refreshments.

shrines. A road leads to its summit, with rest stations every few miles, but it can rarely be ascended except in the Spring. for later on towards Winter its top is buried in clouds, and fierce winds rage for days together, even when all is quiet below. Many travelers have been swept off from its sides like feathers

Mt. Fuji.

and no one ever knew what became of them; also for a greater part of the year its top is covered with snow, so that it can not be ascended. Fuji is one of the wonders of Japan, and no picture is complete without it. Its fadeless grandeur is the crowning sight of the landscape visible from thirteen provinces. Incoming vessels from abroad have their decks crowded with eager passengers skimming the horizon for the first view, and a cry of rapture goes up when through its fickle clouds it condescends to reveal its noble form to "barbarian" eyes.

Dai Butsu.
(Great Buddha.)

The scenery around Hakone itself is of surpassing loveliness. The straw-thatched roofs of the village, nestling among the hills, with its one single street, the mirror-like waters of the lake reflecting the delightful pictures above and around it, all furnish a rich feast for the traveler's eyes.

Just before reaching Yokohama Matsuda turned aside from the road for a few miles to visit with his mother the fast perishing ruins of Kamakura, the former capital of Yoritomo, under whose reign its population numbered 500,000 souls. But it is now little more than a sand heap. Nothing of importance remains except a great bronze image of Buddha, which, with the great bell of Kioto, is the only substantial relic of the Golden Days of Buddhism under the first Shogun. The image is called *Dai Butsu* (Great Buddha), and represents the "Light of Asia" sitting in *Nirvana* upon a lotus blossom, the symbol of tranquillity. Aside from the similar statue at Nara, near Kioto, this is the greatest piece of art of its kind in Japan. Though in a sitting posture it is fifty feet high, and its inside forms a large temple. Tourists often climb into his lap and sit on his great folded thumbs to have their photographs taken. The face is one of serene repose. Earthquakes have caused him to nod on his lotus throne, and tidal waves from the sea twice have rolled over him, destroying the great wooden temples that had been erected above him, but still he sits in undisturbed repose, a sleep dreamless and eternal, oblivious to all the throes of nature and the pangs of existence. So sleeps Buddha; so hope to sleep all who follow him in the "path of illumination."

The devout old woman gazed reverently upon the dead peacefulness of that bronze face and longed for the time when she, too, could be like him, insensible to all outward impressions, undisturbed by the might-

Yokohama and Harbor.

iest physical disasters; no life nor death, no recognition of friends, no separation from loved ones—only Lethe! No wonder *hara-kiri* is so common. Where there is no dread of future punishment annihilation is preferable to a life that is often miserable at best.

Returning to the main road, Matsuda and his party proceeded as far as Kanagawa, on the shore of Yedo Bay, sixteen miles from Tokio. Here they left the Tokaido and crossed a causeway over a marshy lagoon, two miles to the other side, where Yokohama had sprung up like an enchantment of Alladin, but it had come to stay. Yokohama had been an insignificant fishing village, where it was decided that the first treaty port should be opened. Lying just across the arm of the bay from the town of Kanagawa, which it supplied with fish, it got its name from its position—*Yoko* (across), *hama* (strand).

CHAPTER IX.

LIFE IN YOKOHAMA.

FROM a fishing village Yokohama had suddenly been transformed into a metropolis, one of the great trading ports of the world. The government expended liberal sums of money in making it a convenient and pleasant place. An elevated causeway was constructed across the strip of water, connecting it with Kanagawa and the Tokaido, and hence with Tokio. Junks from Osaka, the Inland Sea, and all ports of the empire now made it one of their regular stopping places. Immense steamers, resembling great floating cities, made monthly trips between here and San Francisco. All vessels sailing between China and the United States landed here, both going and coming. In fact, Yokohama was now shaking hands with the whole world.

The city is built upon a low plain, nearly one square mile in area, and on the sides and top of the range of hills that surround it. On a picturesque promontory of one of these, south of the town, is the "Bluff" where the foreign residents have their homes. These are beautiful villas and cottages surrounded by luxuriant gardens, and with smoothly paved streets in front. In the cool of the day splendid carriages drawn by fine imported horses dash by in all directions, filled with gay pleasure seekers. The view

Art Gallery.

from the Bluff is entrancing beyond description. First always you see Fuji's peerless cone with its changing hues, if the day is clear. Then the nearer landscape attracts you. The hills are terraced to the top and cultivated to the highest stage of perfection with perfectly kept Japanese gardens. Beyond the

Street in Yokohama.

creek that skirts the hill is a serpentine strip of lowland, reclaimed from the ancient marshes, and converted into fields of green growing rice, surrounded with deep ditches that collect the water and irrigate the fields as they need it. The hills all around are dotted with their neat European houses, each upon its own well kept terrace, and surrounded with vistas of native trees and semi-tropical vegetation of every variety.

The city itself is divided into several different quarters. Europeans (including Americans always) are grouped together in a prescribed limit called the "Concession." Here they have their business houses, hotels and clubs. The principal business street was the Bund, or Sea Road, which runs along the stone wall by the shore. Later the business has mostly been transferred to Main Street.

Besides the native town there is also a "Chinatown," where ordinary Celestials and pompous "Compradores" live. These last are the Chinese brokers and commission merchants who absolutely control the markets of the city, everything having to pass through their hands.

The bay is dotted with small craft, black merchant vessels, white men-of-war, red canal tugs, and an occasional steamer for a distant port. When a foreign vessel arrives there is a scene of the wildest confusion and indescribable uproar to one not familiar with such. Swift moving *sampans* propelled by half-naked coolies, whose heads are covered with the omnipresent blue-and-white cotton towel, dart around seeking passengers to be conveyed to the shore, since large steamers can not reach the landing. Little tugs smoke and puff as they plow back and forth with the mail. The landing is covered with *jinrikisha*, whose clamoring drivers (?) each propose to do you the best service possible.

At first sight our new comers were shocked at what they saw. The city was too much Japanese to be foreign, and yet too foreign to be recognized as Japanese. The charm of native life was all gone, and there was not enough of real foreign life to recom-

Basket Maker on way to Market.

mend it. Then the "barbarians" themselves, how horrid! How strange to see strong-looking men with light hair and blue eyes, and whiskers all over their faces—it was disgusting! The Japanese all have intensely black hair and eyes, and at that time were smooth-faced. The manners of the foreigners, too, were revolting in the extreme. One burly Englishman was seen deliberately to kick a cooly and swear at him! They all seemed bullies, and from a native standpoint they were. Time is too short, even if they felt disposed, for English and American tradesmen to get down on their faces when they meet. They are too practical to spend needless time in debasing self and exalting the party addressed. Yet, while many ruffians had found their way hither, as they always do at such places, there were enough of the better class to show to the unprejudiced native that not all were worthy to be called "foreign devils," as they had been named.

Whatever may have been the first impressions of a native visiting Yokohama, his keen intelligence and quick perception soon caused him to see the great advantages that had come with the foreigner, and he was stimulated to enter enthusiastically into making the best of his opportunities.

Matsuda procured a neat little house and garden in the Japanese quarter and settled down to live as near in his former style as was in keeping with his present circumstances. His duties were not burdensome, since he was only required to act as a kind of head policeman to see that the conditions of the treaties, the custom laws, etc., were properly carried out. It was more a position of honor than otherwise.

A new and grave problem now arose. The oldest two boys, Ichiro and Saburo, were now old enough to be in school, being seventeen and thirteen respectively. Their father had determined to give them a thorough education according to the foreign methods, so that they could take their place among the rising young men of the country and become useful citizens. The trouble was that there was no school in reach, except one taught by a Christian missionary, and Matsuda still shared in the national and inherited hatred against the "Corrupt Sect."

Recently the edicts against Christianity had been revived and new orders given to enforce them. It was found since the opening of the country that near Nagasaki, in spite of all the horrible persecutions and the diligent secret detective service employed for so long a time, there were about ten thousand who now avowed themselves as adherents to the forbidden faith. Through two and a half centuries they had clung to the dim traditions of a Saviour who could lead them to a better life. True, they knew next to nothing of practical Christianity, and nothing of the Bible, yet their open profession caused a renewal of the edicts. When the government undertook to enforce them, however, the foreign powers resented it as an offense against them, since they were from Christian lands. This led to considerations that resulted in religious freedom for Japan. A number of American teachers who had been employed to teach in the interior also had much to do in securing freedom of conscience for the natives. When the government inserted in the contract a clause by which they agreed not to open their mouths on religious questions they refused to sign them and the objectionable words were stricken out. They now taught the Bible openly in their schools and tried to impress upon the students the fact that Christianity and education should go together.

It was plain to all who considered the matter that the religion of these teachers was very different from that taught by the Jesuits of the Sixteenth Century. It encouraged to peace, required submission to rulers, and sought to enlighten the people; whereas, the Catholic religion had held the people in ignorance of even the fundamental truths of religion, and had sought to overthrow the government by intrigue.

Aside from his inborn prejudice against Christianity, Matsuda had no longer any religious convictions to speak of. During the busy and stormy scenes of the past few years he had scarcely given it a thought, more than to see that his mother had its privileges. The popular superstitions of the people he now recognized as folly. Buddhism had lost its place as a national religion, and the Emperor had destroyed the sanctity of Shinto by appearing in open daylight as a mere man. It really seemed to many people now that religion amounted to but little anyhow. It was certain that the existing religions could show nothing to recommend them except a few bells, images and temples of wonderful carvings. As to the life of the people, there were more than 32,000,-000 who were degraded from the rank of citizenship to that of semi-brutes, many of them being considered as "not-human." Matsuda, with all his prejudice, could see that Christianity was gradually bringing the extreme high and low classes to a common level. It had come with the new civilization, and if it could improve matters he had no objection to it. He cared nothing about the spiritual influence it claimed. He was beginning to believe, with a great many more of his country, that everything spiritual was simply superstition, and hence looked upon the matter from a purely rationalistic standpoint.

After some months of personal observation of the lives and characters of the Christian teachers, he decided that his children were not likely to be injured by them, and so he placed the two boys under the care of Mr. Miller, while Mrs. Miller came to teach Toki and Chrysanthemum at home. Having disposed of the matter to his satisfaction he gave it no more attention, but devoted himself to his business and let things go on in their own way with no uneasiness as to the result. He had always forbidden the nurses to excite the superstitions of the children by telling them the popular nursery tales about fox spirits, wind imps, ghosts, etc., and he was glad to learn that the Christians also discouraged such things, for from time immemorial both women and children had been educated into a painful dread of imaginary hobgoblins that were supposed to be in the air, and of the great fish in the center of the earth, the shaking of whose tail caused the earthquakes.

Toki's ideas as to Christianity were much more favorable than her husband's. True, she had been frightened when a child by the very mention of the "Barbarian Criminal God," Yasu, but now her quick intuition had taken in the situation at a glance, after having observed the state of affairs at Yokohama. She delighted in the new order of things and entered with great zeal upon the studies proposed by Mrs. Miller.

It should be remembered that while woman in Japan is nominally a drudge and inferior to man, yet in reality she often rises above him in the intellectual scale, and as a general thing receives more respect than she does in most eastern countries. Nearly all the standard popular books that are read by everybody in Japan, such as our Robinson Crusoe, were written by women. They knew only the native dialect, whereas would-be scholars affected Chinese as many of ours have affected Latin, and as no one can write a masterpiece in any save his own tongue, their works are comparative failures, while those of their less pretentious wives will live forever.

Toki was well trained intellectually, and made good progress in learning English and in gaining a knowledge of the Bible, which she taught to her children. She was surprised that so many ladies who called upon her expressed such undisguised contempt for missionaries. True, they were hairy, and uncouth in their manners, from a Japanese standpoint, but she thought allowance should be made for the differences of custom in the land whence they came. Some spoke lightly of the arrival of a new missionary as a joke for the amusement of a dinner party. When any one so far forgot himself in this hybrid community as to fail in some point of etiquette he would excuse himself on the grounds that he had been among missionaries and had learned bad manners from them. This always pained Toki, and she wished that the missionaries, for their own sake, would try to adapt themselves to the customs of the country.

CHAPTER X.

A PILGRIMAGE TO NIKKO.

GRANDMOTHER KIMURA took no interest in the new-fashioned ways into which the country had fallen. She was too old to learn a new religion or new customs. So she spent her days in quiet devotion, with an occasional pilgrimage to some holy shrine. It had long been her cherished desire to visit Nikko, the tomb and shrine of Iyeyasu, one of the most famous places in Japan. So remarkable is its splendor that it has given rise to a proverb: "He who has not seen Nikko has no right to say *kekko!*—(beautiful)."

Nikko is the great summer resort for the higher classes of Tokio. Here many of them seek refuge from the heat of the flat and blistering streets, and lodge in the ancient temples or camp under the cool, solemn shade of giant trees. It was now near the close of the hot season, and many were leaving, but Matsuda found the family of a government official who were going from Yokohama to spend a few days, so he consigned his mother to their care, and arranged for her to go before the winter season should come on.

Nikko is about one hundred miles north of Tokio. The recently completed railroad was not then constructed, so they had to go thirty miles by boat, and the remaining seventy in *jinrikisha*. The great road which leads from the landing to the tomb is a marvel of engineering. It is graded almost as perfectly as a railroad, cutting through hills and built up across valleys. It was constructed over two hundred years ago, and made as even as possible in order that the bodies of the great shoguns that were borne over it

Sacred Bridge.

might have a smooth and safe journey to their splendid, but mournfully solemn resting place. On each side, and arching overhead, are rows of tall and ancient cryptomeria trees that guard, like lines of grim soldiery, this imperial highway to the grave. Some of the trees are four or five feet in diameter, and one hundred and fifty feet high. By their roots run streams of clear mountain water, always refreshing and musical with their rippling flow. The road itself has been canonized, and hence is sacred. It is very smooth and hard, having been trodden by the feet of many generations. Tea-houses are abundant on this road, as on all others. The coolies stopped every few miles for refreshments, and to renew their straw sandals. The road was literally strewn with these cast off remnants of foot-gear from the feet of many runners, this having been an unusually busy season, and the straw soles not enduring for more than a few miles' run.

Dashing through the long sloping street on which the town of Nikko was strung, crossing a beautiful hill a little beyond, they came to a rushing stream spanned by two bridges, one of plain wood, which was crossed by *jinrikisha* and foot passengers, the other an enclosed structure of red lacquer highly ornamented, which could be crossed only by the shogun in former times, and now by the Emperor. Here the cooly turned in the shafts and, as he mopped his grinning face, exclaimed ecstatically,

"NIKKO, NIKKO!"

Sure enough, beyond the stream was a thickly wooded hill-side, near the top of which, at the end of long, dim avenues of tall cryptomerias, stood a towering pagoda and the imposing gateways to the two temples built in front of the graves of Iyeyasu and Iyemitsu, his grandson, who completed the structures. No one save the Emperor dares to touch the sacred bridge covered with its red lacquer and ornamented with its many tips and plates of brass. When Gen. Grant stood before it, the Emperor, desiring to show the highest possible honor to his guest, ordered the gates to be thrown open that the distinguished ex-President might pass over. But the modest soldier had no claims to divinity by which to justify such an act, which to the people would seem a desecration, so he politely declined.

No book has ever yet satisfactorily described Nikko. In fact, it is beyond the power of words to express. No photography can reproduce it. Its solemn shadows, its velvety mossy banks, its crystal streams of trickling water whose music is unceasing, its varieties of color and exquisite combinations of shades and tints, its solemn silence mournfully musical with rustling leaves and gurgling waters, can not be reproduced except in the imaginative memory of the departed visitor who shuts his eyes and sees afresh the scenes that bewildered him when he stood among them in person. You can see, hear, and feel Nikko, but you can not describe it. So I shall only point out some of the most prominent features, and leave the rest to the reader's imagination or to the satisfaction of a future visit.

Mrs. Kimura and her party crossed the plain wooden bridge, passed a little scarlet-colored shrine at the edge of the wood, and entered the avenue leading up the steep hill to the gate of the Iyeyasu temple, which is the most important of the two. The tall cryptomerias look like needle-shaped pines, their sides touching overhead. They stand on high mossy banks on each side of the stone-flagged pathway. In the center of the path, running in a channel cut for it, is a glassy cool stream always laughing and darting by as if anxious to reach the bottom to greet new visitors. On one side they passed the walls of a great monastery. At the summit of this ascent is a

Approach to the Temple.

lofty *torii* of immense granite posts, three feet in diameter and over twenty-seven feet high, with a heavy up-curving cross-piece. Through this commanding entrance, emblematical of national pride and patriotism, they entered upon a broad stone piazza. Around this were one hundred and eighteen magnificent stone lanterns on immense pedestals of granite, each bearing inscriptions of the posthumous title of Iyeyasu, the name of the *daimyo* who gave it, and a legend of its origin. To the left, on the stone platform, rose a tall pagoda of five stories, its walls gleaming with red lacquer, its railings and roof trimmings covered with brass, every angle hung with bells, a wonderfully curved roof on top, and its bottom story painted with twelve animals representing the signs of the zodiac. To the right, in a cryptomeria glade reached by a short flight of moss-covered steps, stands a little gem of a temple surrounded with deep grass dotted with flowers. Inside of it are rich paintings and a great bell, it having been provided in order that worship might be continued here in case the larger temples should be closed.

After passing under the great stone *torii* the party stood on the level platform for a few moments to look at the scenes without, then proceeded straight ahead up a flight of crumbling mossy steps to the magnificent gateway leading to the first court of the temple. The gateway itself, with its heavy curved roof and its exquisite carvings, might have held an artist enraptured for hours, were it not for a glimpse of what lay beyond, making the beholder too impatient to remain to see what could be viewed from the outside any day. Inside they passed through a pebbled court enclosed by a red wooden wall. Here were three magnificent treasure houses for the temples, containing all the things that the great Shogun called his own and prized in this life. There is also a handsome stable in which is kept the sacred white

Albino pony for the use of the gods. Crossing the court on the walk of flag stones, the visitors stood before a great stone water-tank covered by a canopy, gorgeous in its colors of scarlet and gold, and supported by twelve stone pillars. The huge block is so accurately leveled that the water, rising up from the bottom, glides down the sides so evenly as to look like a solid cube of ice. Near this also is a building containing the Buddhist Scriptures, numbering nearly seven thousand volumes. They were arranged in a large revolving case, and the priest told the visitors that if they wished to gain the merit of having read them all they might each take hold and revolve the case three times, and they should receive full credit of knowing the sacred canon by heart. They all obeyed in great sincerity and passed on with a feeling of deep satisfaction.

They now passed under a noble bronze *torii* leading to another paved pathway up the hill. Three tiers of stone steps rose in succession. On each side was a stone balustrade and a row of iron lanterns, the head of the steps being protected by stone lions leaping down on each side. Crowning the third flight is the indescribable Yomeimon gateway, unsurpassed by any the world has ever seen. Visitors stand before it for hours at a time, day after day, and gaze upon it with increasing rapture. The matchless white stone columns which support its immense roof are crowned by capitals of wonderfully carved heads of a mythical animal of the Middle Ages. One of the pillars was purposely placed upside down

Yomeimon Gateway.

A PILGRIMAGE TO NIKKO.

to avert evil, the architect being afraid that the jealousy of the gods might break out upon him if he completed to perfection so heavenly a structure. Above is a beetling balcony with a wonderful balustrade supported by carved groups of playing chil-

Nearer View of the Yomeimon.

dren. The cornices are carvings of ancient sages, and the superb roof crowning all is supported by dragons' heads perfectly carved. So much in general; it is impossible to describe the infinite details of its exquisite workmanship, its richly painted beams, its life-like imagery in carvings, its gorgeousness of coloring in gold, red and glittering white.

The awe-stricken group held their breath and passed through to the next court. Each passage was from splendor to splendor. Could it be that the departed warrior had an idea of degrees in heaven that he arranged the approach to his tomb in such a succession of progressive glories? The visitors passed through this last court so oppressed with the view of its magnificence that they were anxious to reach the climax—the temple—when they could feel relieved that there was nothing grander yet to be seen. Too much splendor is absolutely painful to those not enough accustomed to it to be indifferent toward it. They pressed through the remaining gate, no less magnificent, though smaller than the other, and then paused with reverent awe, for they stood under the dim shadow of the shed that leads into the golden temple itself. Here they pulled off their shoes and fell upon their faces in worship, tossing a few coins wrapped in paper upon the temple floor. Inside it is sufficient to say that the climax of Japanese art in its Golden Age is represented. Its floors are covered with the finest lacquer ever laid. Its finely paneled ceiling is covered with golden dragons on a richly blue lacquered background. Gilded doors mercifully conceal the "severe magnificence" of four inner rooms. The roof is an upheaving sea of carvings, gables and multiplied grandeurs. After seeing all that was visible without and in the corridors the pilgrims breathlessly approached the inner shrine, half

Golden Shrine of Iyeyasu.

fearing to look upon what they naturally expected to be the concentration of every possible splendor. splendor. They entered and beheld—a black lacquer table and upon it a round metal mirror, reflection of the Sun Goddess! The Mikado had recently removed all the Buddhistic pomps, and replaced them by the plainer symbols of the restored Shinto faith.

Still where is Iyeyasu?

The priest conducted them back through the gate that led to the next court, turned to the right, passed through a little canopied door that opened upon a flight of two hundred and forty mossy stone steps leading to the top of the hill immediately behind and above the temple. At the top was another lofty *torii*, another shrine, a great stone-and-bronze tomb on which was a bronze urn, and under it the dust of the great Shogun. As were the temple and tomb of Iyeyasu, so were those of Iyemitsu, only little less magnificent.

Iyeyasu's tomb is emblematic of his life. Through universal victory and from glory to glory his pathway had led, then terminated in death—silent, hopeless, everlasting death—Nirvana.

In front and below were all that human art at its best could do to adorn his resting place. All around, even at noon-day, Nature has thrown a pall of perpetual twilight. Great evergreen cryptomerias, with their somber foliage meeting high over head, shut out the sunlight, and their tall, straight bodies look like the cloistered columns of a vast temple in whose lofty ceiling of dark green foliage and distant shady

A PILGRIMAGE TO NIKKO.

colonnades the hushed voices of the worshipers awake no echoes. No flowers bloom in its sunless mossy soil, no bird sings its notes of joy. The water trickles ceaselessly, the leaves rustle gently in the scarcely perceptible breeze that sifts through. Overhead a solitary rook cries with a mournful croak befitting the scene, far and near are mossy shrines and steps and silent Buddhas. These are all the visitors saw to remind them of Japan's greatest statesman. What must be the emotions of a sensitive soul when viewing such a scene for the first time! A foreigner who was just leaving, and who did not have to depend upon the Buddhist religion for salvation, remarked, "I am overcome with reverence for a religion that can produce a work like that and teach the people to appreciate it." Alas, if religion were only the appreciation of art how easy to be saved and to teach men so! A pious missionary

Tomb of Iyeyasu.

turned away with a feeling almost of despair. "Alas!" he said, "who can combat successfully a religion that inspires such strong emotions!"

As for Grandmother Kimura, she stood speechless, pensive. She thought, "All this is overpowering to us pilgrims, but what effect does it have on dead Iyeyasu? After all, does the life of the greatest man lead through all his funereal splendor to perish in solitude amid the dashing of waterfalls, the croaking of rooks, and the sighing of ancient pines? But even Dai Butsu promises no better. It is only Nirvana. What was it that the foreign lady said to Toki and Kiku the other day about a land beyond that is fairer than our brightest day dreams; a city brighter than the sun; mansions of heavenly splendor where families are reunited and live forever without sorrow or parting, praising God, the Life of their souls? I paid but little attention to it then, but surely if that be true it is better than this. Better a soul living in bliss beyond than a body mouldering in silent splendor here. Oh, I wish I had listened to what she said and let her read to me from the Book that told about it.

The party remained for several days, visiting shrine after shrine, and admiring the endless beauties that daily opened to their bewildered eyes. But Grandmother Kimura had lost interest. She wanted to learn about the other world of which she had heard only a word, and which the emptiness of all she saw made all the more desirable. It was with a sigh of relief that she finally joined the party on the way home. SHE WENT HOME PRAYING.

CHAPTER XI.

AMONG THE AINU.

COMPLAINTS had recently come to the government about abuses practiced upon the Ainu, in Yezo, by Japanese traders. Matsuda, who was now fully acquainted with all the regulations, was despatched to go to Yezo with a posse of mounted police and see that the laws were properly executed, and that the Ainu received justice.

These hairy savages were the aborigines of Japan, who, being a mild and inoffensive people, were driven from place to place by the more powerful and warlike Japanese until they were finally colonized in Yezo, the northern island. Hitherto they had been looked upon as dogs, and were called "Aino" (Mongrel, Cur), and treated as if they had been brutes. But recently the government had undertaken to protect them, and found that they made peaceable and law-abiding citizens when they had the opportunity. The Japanese traders, however, were in the habit of making them drunk and then taking all kinds of mean advantage of them.

The Ainu are a very timid people, and have such a fearful dread of others, especially of their conquerors, the Japanese, that Matsuda found great difficulty in coming near them and gaining their confidence. Gradually, however, by presents and assurances of kindness, he so gained their esteem that they were glad to have him visit their poor huts, and became quite free in conversation with him, a thing that had never been accomplished before. He had been commissioned to find out all he could about them and make an official report to the government in regard to their numbers, their manners and customs, and their religion, very little being known about them beyond the fact that they were there, a savage community. Hitherto no one had considered them as human beings, but now the government had made them citizens and was endeavoring to get a census of them. The time had been when as a *samurai* Matsuda would have cut down with his sword any one of the poor wretches whom he met, with as little compunction of conscience as he would have felt in slaying a wolf. But now he had overcome his prejudice, and was glad to do them a service. Leaving his men to guard the frontier and keep the peace, he proceeded into the thickest settled part of the country and took up his abode with one of the strongest chiefs.

The house of Chief Bura, Matsuda's host, was like all other Ainu houses, only larger than those of the other men of the village. It was composed almost entirely of reeds, and like a Japanese house, the roof was put on first. Posts were set in the ground for the corners and supports. Poles were strapped on the top, middle and bottom of these as cross pieces to which the long reeds were fastened in a vertical position, tied on with bark. The long rafters for the steep roof were tied on to the top poles before the walls were fastened on, and the roof was thatched with straw. An opening was left in the south end for a door; two others, protected by rude shutters, were left near the eaves, one in the east side, the other in the south. Then you have a house. They have no floor nor furniture, for they need none. An oblong opening in the ground in the center of the room serves for fireplace, kitchen and dining-room. Here at one end the fire is made to warm the inmates; at the other end, from a suspended hook, hangs a black pot in which the rice is cooked for the daily meals. Much ceremony is observed around this fireside. Each one of the family is provided with a special place to sit according to rank, a seat of honor being reserved for visitors, which was filled by Matsuda, who sat on the bearskin rug prepared for him. The ceremonious reception of visitors is always conducted by the fireplace. When dinner time comes the mother opens the pot hanging over the fire and helps the family to rice, putting a ladleful in each little lacquer bowl, which is waved gracefully back and forth in an act of worship before partaking.

The east window is sacred, since it looks toward the Rising Sun. Nothing is ever thrown out of it, and it is considered a great desecration for any one to look in through it. Before it every morning the old chief offered his prayers. Just without this window was a scaffold, which served as an altar. On it were bears' heads and other offerings. The Ainu have no temples, but around a sacred spot they place white wands stuck in the ground and whittled at the top into long shavings that are left to hang down. These are called *inao*. A man who has no *inao* is most unfortunate, and can not hope for the favor of gods or men. Some travelers had reported that they worshiped these *inao* as gods. But they have no images or visible objects of worship, as Matsuda found, and the wands are simply offerings that are believed to be most acceptable to the gods. When in a storm at sea *inao* are cut from switches always kept for the purpose, and thrown into the water to propitiate the goddess of the sea and induce her to quiet the storm. The bear is the most highly prized treasure they ever possess. They go on a hunt every year, and when a bear is killed there is great rejoicing in the whole village, and a feast follows with much drinking of *sake*, itself an act of worship. A cub is usually kept in a cage and fattened for such a feast when the hunt fails. To offer a bear's head to the gods is to make a most acceptable sacrifice.

Matsuda's bed was on one side of the room. Four short forks were driven into the ground to support poles, on which rough boards were laid and covered with bearskins. This made a hard, but not uncomfortable bed for a Japanese who had slept on a mat on the floor all his life.

Matsuda noticed that the women were treated with much less respect than the women of his own country. They were not recognized as human beings, not allowed to have any part in any of the men's feasts or even worship, the men being afraid for the women to pray, believing them to be in league with evil spirits. The women do all the work, while the men hunt, fish or lie around and drink. When they came in they always made very respectful salutations to the men and walked out backwards, a woman never being allowed to turn her back on a man. The younger women were often very pretty, with clear, rich complexions, but by the revolting process of tattooing they soon became hideous. Broad black stripes were tattooed around the mouth, and extended from the corners, causing the mouth to seem to extend from ear to ear. The eyebrows were also connected across the forehead.

Most of the men were really fine looking, their long flowing beards giving them a patriarchal appearance. Their voices were soft, and their language more musical than the Japanese. They were gentle and scrupulously polite in their manners. Although they show no special regard for their wives, they are very affectionate to their children, often caressing them by the hour.

On no account will an Ainu approach a grave. The spirit of the departed is believed to hover near for a while, and takes fearful revenge upon any one who intrudes. For this reason the dead are always buried far away in the forest, and a sign is placed over the grave so that no one may approach it without warning. The men are specially afraid of the ghosts of the women, who are believed to have gone to the evil world. The poor creatures are so badly mistreated in this world that it is but natural for their abusers to fear that they will take revenge when they

Aina Men.

become spirits and can do it without being discovered.

The Ainu never wash their bodies nor change their clothes except on occasions of a feast or worship. The usual seasons of worship are at the bear feast following a hunt, at a house-warming, at a burial, or any great event that seems to demand it. Worship consists in offering *inao* and drinking *sake*. On such occasions they drink till in a state of beastly intoxication, in which they lie for several days, sincerely believing that in this way they are serving the gods in the most acceptable manner. They can not conceive of how the gods can be worshiped without *sake*, which is so highly prized among themselves.

The people all greatly reverence the memory of Yoshitsune, Yoritomo's badly mistreated brother, who is believed to have spent his exile in their country and to have taught them several useful arts. His name figures largely in their legends, and there is a shrine erected to him at Piratori. It is not for worship, since they never worship images, but serves as a memorial of a grateful people to their only benefactor. Their own dead they never mention on account of the dread they have of them. For this reason they can have no history. There is no written language, and their oral legends are mostly about gods and heroes of other times.

Matsuda became greatly interested in ascertaining their views of God and the future state, which were so different from anything that he had ever heard among the Buddhists. He found that they believe in one Supreme God and a multitude of inferior gods. They also believe in evil as well as good deities. The ancestor of their race is greatly reverenced, though not worshiped. Both men and animals are believed to have immortal souls, and all will be judged alike. The spirits of dead animals guard their living masters.

It is a very rare thing that the people will talk to a stranger about their religious beliefs, but on the night before Matsuda left, old chief Bura had imbibed a liberal amount of *sake*, and, as a consequence, was unusually religious and in an affable frame of mind. When the family had all gathered around the firehole at night, each sitting in his own proper place on the ground, Matsuda on his bearskin at the east end, the subject of ghosts came up. Matsuda ventured to ask what were their views of the future life, having seen that they entertained different ideas from any he had ever heard. After much rubbing of his hands and stroking of his long curly beard in deference to his distinguished guest, old Bura began to relate a story:

"In a great hill many miles away there is a dark cavern. Through this gloomy passage the spirits of the dead enter the other world. A man had lost his father and mother. Tradition said that they had gone through the cavern to the world beyond. This man was not afraid. He carried a strong bow and a quiver full of arrows. He said he would visit that land whence none had ever returned and find his parents. Fearlessly he plunged into the darkness.

Blindly he stumbled on. The way was long and dark. Finally he saw a little light far away. At last it grew larger, and he saw that he was approaching the entrance to the cavern from the other side. He stepped out into the dazzling light of a greater sun than that of this world. On a broad plain basking in the radiant sunlight were many villages. He saw that the people live there as they do here, only happier and better. More birds sang with sweeter music, and the woods looked greener.

"The man went on. He came to a large village in which his father lived. The dogs ran wildly here and there. They smelt a ghost, but could not see him. In that world a man from this world is to them like a ghost is with us. He found his father. He was sitting by the door in the sun. The man spoke to him. He asked him to go back to his home and to his children. The old man was frightened. He looked up and down and all around. He heard a voice, but could see nothing. Others came. They heard and were distressed.

"The man saw that he only frightened them, and that they were better off there than here. Then he started to leave them there and return home. This time the passage seemed darker and colder. In the darkness he met a soul descending. He spoke to it, but the soul shrieked with fear and rushed on. It was so dark that he could not see the soul's face. He arrived at home. He went to tell his nearest neighbor what he had seen. They said his neighbor had just died, and so that was his soul which he had met

116   IN THE LAND OF THE SUNRISE.

in the dark passage. The man shivered and went to his home. So there is no good from following the dead or inquiring after them. Let them alone."*

---

*For information about these wonderful people see "THE AINU OF JAPAN," by Bachelor. They number about 17,000, and are becoming extinct from dissipation and internal wars. A mission has been established among them. The native church now numbers 30 members.

CHAPTER XII.

A PAINFUL DISCOVERY.

THE government was now making active endeavors to elevate the lower classes, who constituted a greater portion of the people. While the upper classes had attained a high state of civilization, still the masses, on account of the oppressions which they had suffered, had sunken to a correspondingly low extreme. New laws recently enacted by the government required the people to wear clothing, a thing which millions had not been accustomed to do, except when compelled by cold weather. Public bathhouses were now required to furnish separate apartments for men and women. Schools were being established in all the towns as fast as possible. Railways and ships added to the facilities for transmitting knowledge of the world and of the sciences. Newspapers were becoming abundant, and were read by thousands. Still only a beginning had been made, and many millions were yet steeped in ignorance and poverty.

Having finished his work in Yezo, Matsuda was commissioned by the government to make a tour of the northern interior of the main island on his way home, for the purpose of learning the real condition and needs of the people, and of enforcing any of the new regulations that might be neglected by the local officials. His armed guard of mounted police was to accompany him, and aid in impressing the people with the importance of abiding by the new regulations.

Hundreds of foreign travelers annually visiting Japan, who simply touch at a few of the treaty ports, ride on the Tokaido, and visit a few shrines and famous places like Nikko and Ise, where they meet only the higher classes of people, return home, and, as far as they know, write truthfully of the beauties of Japanese scenery, the attractiveness of the women and the homes, and the charm of native life, with the wonderful advancements visible in the cities and larger towns. Hence their readers fancy that all Japan is a perfect Eden, where no sorrow ever comes, and no want is ever known. Alas, how little they know of the whole truth! For where there are a few hundred thousand of the enlightened there are many millions who are in the grossest spiritual darkness, and suffering with poverty and disease. To let them know that they were now looked upon as "human" and that human responsibilities were placed upon them, was the aim of the wise young ruler. Hence the mission of Matsuda through the interior.

Although Matsuda was a *samurai*, and, as a soldier, had been over much of the country, he was not prepared for the scenes of distress that awaited him.

Frequently as he and his party passed along the highway they were met by naked coolies pulling *jinrikisha*. Immediately upon sight of the officers the poor fellows would scud behind their vehicles, scramble into their clothes, then prostrate themselves upon the ground in the utmost reverence until the dreaded uniforms were out of sight. This served to show that, while many were acquainted with the laws, there was not enough education of public sentiment to enforce them.

The peasants are strangely superstitious and improvident, even reckless of their lives. The character of the land and the phenomena of Nature fully explain their peculiar disposition. Many things conspire to foster their superstitions and to weaken their confidence in the stability of human life, or even of Nature itself, and yet their refined natures are also a product of their environment.

The picturesque beauty of the landscape is unsurpassed by that of any country in the world. Its blue skies, bluer lakes and bays, sparkling rivulets, snowy mountain crests, fleecy clouds, green hills, and peaceful valleys, with a luxuriance of flowers everywhere, might account for the artistic taste, the gentleness, and the love for the beautiful that is almost universal, even among the most degraded. Politeness and gentleness seem inborn, though their warriors have sometimes committed acts of the most savage cruelty.

There are also natural causes for their superstitions. For in the midst of all the loveliness of Nature they are never free from her most dreaded terrors. The land is volcanic in its origin. If there is a bright green landscape in a peaceful valley, there is above it a dark frowning cliff that grinds its rocks with horrible sounds when in the throes of an earthquake, and often tumbles its boulders down upon the homes of the helpless inhabitants. From its dark caverns these awful groanings sound like angry demons at war, and hence the people believe that they are inhabited by evil spirits. Those snow-clad mountain peaks are liable at any time to explode and cover whole districts with mud, lava, and burning cinders. The solid earth often trembles beneath them, causing the leaves and the green fruit to tumble from the trees, pebbles to shoot out from the hillsides, and the plains to open with awful rents, into which whole houses are sometimes swallowed up, though such severe shocks are not now so frequent. They believe that there is in the sea under the islands a great fish which shakes its tail when it gets angry, thus causing the earthquake disasters.

Those who live by the sea and daily behold its varied beauty are subjected at the most unexpected times to the violence of great tidal waves that sweep away whole villages and roll inland for many miles over the plains. Again, as if Nature was not content with destroying the foundations of security on land and sea, great periodical typhoons and revolving storms sweep over earth and ocean, leaving hideous wreck and ruin behind them. The people believe they are caused by angry wind imps that live in the clouds and bring disaster when displeased. Each natural disturbance is caused by its special demon that has the control over it. They are especially afraid of the foxes that live in the dens of the mountains, believing that they are the incarnations of evil spirits. Immense artificial marshes are made

A PAINFUL DISCOVERY.   121

for the cultivation of rice. These are covered with manure, then flooded with water. The land is soon covered with the stench of decaying matter, and at night the gases rise in bubbles to the surface, burst and float away in luminous balls like phantom Will-o'-the-wisps. These are believed to be the eyes of the fox spirits trying to allure people to follow them. Horrible stories are told to the children in the nursery about bad people who followed the lights and were lost or horribly mangled. A man followed the light into the woods one night. There he found a most beautiful woman, who walked before him and beckoned him on. Blinded by her beauty he followed, till suddenly she changed into a huge fox and seized him in strong hairy paws that crushed his bones, while the long sharp teeth were gnashed in his face. When released he dragged himself home, but was crippled and misshapened for life. Hence worship is paid to the fox, and shrines are erected to him. Enlightened people now forbid the nurses to tell such stories to their children, but they are still believed in by millions.

Early one morning, while still in the mountains, Matsuda and his party were startled by a terrific explosion that shook the earth so that they could scarcely stand. A vast cloud of smoke and vapor arising from a mountain several miles away showed that a sleeping volcano had exploded. The people were terror-stricken, as they had cause to be, but Matsuda, who was interested in examining into everything that pertained to rural life, rode to the scene with his men and climbed to the crater. Here they looked down upon an awful chaos of sulphurous vapors, boiling mud and floating islands of soil that had fallen in with their burdens of trees and other vegetation. The whole cap of the mountain had been lifted bodily and blown into atoms, no one knew whither. One side of the crater had been blown through, and from it poured a river of mud as broad and deep as the "Father of Waters." At the foot of the mountain a river had been checked by the moving solid wall of mud, and a lake was soon formed that began spreading over the land, flooding a whole village, or that part of it that was left; for scores of houses and their inmates were now buried in twenty feet of hot mud, and there was no need to dig for them, even if there had been time. In the region below where the waters were dammed the people had been cut off from the supply for their rice fields, and unless something could be done soon the new rice crop must perish in the scorching sun, and starvation would be inevitable. Seeing the danger to both sides, Matsuda employed a hundred men to cut a channel through the obstruction at one side where it was sufficiently cool and solid to be dug.

As seen from the mountain-side, the desolation was complete. The objects that had not been destroyed were covered with a mantle of mud and ashes, the landscape preserving its natural features, but ghastly and resembling a corpse covered with the pall of death. As Matsuda stood on the precipice of the crater and peered into the seething abyss below, the great mud wall broke away almost to his feet and tumbled into the boiling cauldron, causing the jelly-like sea to rise and fall with a quivering motion that shook the whole mountain and warned him to beat a hasty retreat. Instinctively he recalled the words of a song he had heard the foreign teacher sing to his children at home in Yokohama:

> "On Christ the solid Rock I stand,
> All other ground is sinking sand."

Pagan that he was, and indifferent to Christianity, he nevertheless mused to himself,

"When earth, sea and sky are unstable and never at rest, what a comfort it would be to a terror-stricken people to find a refuge that abides unmoved to all eternity amid all the wreck and dissolution of creation. There may be such a foundation, but I doubt it."

Leaving the scene of the disaster and proceeding southward, it was found that the landscape soon bore no trace of having ever suffered from above or beneath. Streamlets sparkled in their mossy beds, or dashed in filmy spray from rocky cliffs; the woods were green and echoing with the songs of gayly plumed birds; children played, and all nature seemed to forget that there had ever been a cause for alarm.

Fallen images of Buddha lay on their faces in the tall grass, many of them overgrown with lichen or moss, showing that the disestablished religion was losing power.

Among the crowded villages at the foot of the hills the natural loveliness gave way to human squalor. In the rice swamp half-naked men and women toiled under the burning sun amid the miasmatic vapors, stirring the roots of the young rice with their feet and plucking up weeds with iron hooks. All kinds of insects stung their unprotected backs, while leeches fastened to their feet and legs. After all this toiling they could not afford to eat the rice they raised, but sold it and lived on millet seed and partially decayed dried fish. Matsuda had an opportunity of studying them more closely as a hard rain drove them in under a straw-thatched shed where he had stopped for shelter. The men only wore a waist-cloth, and the children nothing but a piece of metal tied around the neck and inscribed with their names. The women wore only a short skirt reaching from the waist to the knees, or short blue cotton trousers instead, while all had a white and blue cotton towel around their heads. The poisonous insects in the air and the myriads of voracious fleas that infested the dust had covered the exposed parts of their bodies with sores. Some were marked with *"mogusa"* cones, relics of barbarous physicians. When anything ails one an opening is made in the skin of the back and a small taper inserted. This is lighted and allowed to burn slowly until it is consumed beneath the skin, leaving a deep sore that is believed to cure almost all diseases.

All around the shed were ditches filled with liquids that had seeped from the piles of rotting manure, sending off poisonous fumes. Overhead fish were drying and decaying to a proper consistency for use. In one corner huddled shaggy knock-kneed packhorses and pack-cows, the cow being used only as a beast of burden, since neither beef nor butter is known.

Yet, notwithstanding their wretched condition, the people were as gentle as lambs, and as scrupulously polite to each other as the princes of a French court. The middle-aged women bore looks of stolid resignation, or longing hopelessness, though their manners were cheerful. On account of the wretched custom requiring married women to destroy all their charms, when they become homely, as all such do, they lose their husband's affections. Young concubines of attractive features are brought in to take their places, and life has no more joy for the poor cast-off wife. Many of them only continue to live for the sake of their children. The poor creature who has no little ones to love sometimes prefers the oblivion of Nirvana to such a life. Then she puts on her best *kimono*, fills its pocket-like sleeves with stones and leaps from a precipice into a lake. The blue waters cover her secret, and no search is made. She is only one of millions, and perhaps her death is welcomed by others except herself.

The morals of these remote districts still bore the marks of the old feudal age when lying and licentiousness abounded. Nearly all the literature had been putrid, and the whole moral system was corrupt to the core.

With bitter mortification Matsuda prepared his report for the government. He had a justifiable pride in his country, but there was an open sore in peasant life that distressed him. What if a foreigner should penetrate into the interior! He determined to urge immediate steps for reform, and for the elevation of his people, both intellectually and physically.

CHAPTER XIII.

CHRIST IN THE FAMILY.

"O KAERI, O KAERI (He has returned)!" exclaimed the pretty little maid as she rushed to the front of Matsuda's house and opened the sliding *shoji.*

"*Oya* (Papa)!" cried Toki, joyfully. "It is his footstep." Sure enough, there he stood in his uniform, and laying aside his shoes on the porch. Toki knelt on the mat at the door to greet him.

"Welcome home, most honorable husband! I am rejoiced at your safe return."

"*Arigato* (Thanks)! Right glad am I again to hang in your pretty eyes, my sweet wife," he replied, bowing low.

Then came Kiku bounding in with Shiro, rolling from side to side and laughing over her shoulder. They received his warmest greeting, and, swinging to one hand while their mother held to the other sleeve, they followed him into the family room.

"Most august mother, *Ohayo (Good Morning)!* How is the honorable health?"

"I thank you lovingly, most noble son; it is excellent. My only discomfort has been anxiety for your safe return," she replied, with a low bow.

"Ah, you do me too much honor to worry about my unprofitable life. But now that I am come, we will lay aside all such feelings and be happy together again."

While he was talking to his mother Toki was removing his swords and outer coat of uniform.

"Now," she said, as she helped him on with his loose house robe and tied the soft silken girdle about his waist, "you can sit down in comfort while I bring refreshments."

"Ah," said Matsuda as he took his seat on the soft cushion near his mother, "after all the fatigues of travel, and the distress of seeing poverty and misery for months, it is indeed a happy experience to be again at home with the dear loved ones."

Chrysanthemum was fumbling with his coat that he had pulled off. "Papa, what have you brought for us?"

"I beg a thousand pardons, sweet children. Look in my sleeves and you will find cakes and fruits from Tokio for you and Shiro, and a roll of embroidered silks of the latest patterns to make *obi* for you all."

Toki now returned with tea and cakes on the little lacquer table, which she placed on the floor before him, then took her seat on a cushion near by.

As he sipped his tea Matsuda inquired:

"The boys, are they well, and do they progress at school?"

"They are very well, indeed," replied Toki, "and are making most gratifying progress, so the teacher says, and they seem deeply interested. Kiku and I, though only women, have also made progress. We can speak with our teacher in English, and have learned many things that seemed to us wonderful."

At Dinner.

"That is indeed pleasant news," replied her husband. "I am glad to learn of the zeal of the boys, and I never doubted but that the bright minds of my wife and daughter would delight in the new studies. You give me great pleasure. That is what all Japan needs to-day."

A pretty blush suffused Toki's cheeks as she continued:

"Let not my honored husband be angry when he hears other things that may not be so welcome, but we think that now is the time to tell all. Mother, Kiku and I have also learned the new religion."

A shade of annoyance was plainly visible on the princely features of the noble *samurai*, but he did not betray it by speech. It had been his hope and purpose to introduce western culture and material improvement in order to elevate the people and to supplant the old religious superstitions. Now, here in his own home, he found that the "western superstition" had found access. He had hoped to see the country adopt the "practical advantages" and leave the religion out; it was not that which they needed, as far as he could see. But he had already found that, in spite of all opposition, the new religion was spreading, and it really seemed inseparable from the highest civilization. As it was only the women of his family that were inclined toward it, he thought it might be best to let them have their way. It would not hurt them, and women are prone to worship something. All this flashed over his mind in a moment, and when he replied there was only surprise in his tone.

"What, the *Okkasan* too!" looking toward his mother. "I thought she was opposed to everything foreign."

"So I was," replied she, "but having visited the most holy places and having spent several years in sincere devotion to our religion, I find that it can in no wise compare with that of the Christians. Theirs is full of hope and joy. The empty pomp of Nikko can not satisfy a soul that is about to depart from the world with nothing but Nirvana in view. I am supremely happy trusting in the promises of Christ."

"As yet," said Toki, "none of us have been baptized, nor made public profession, We preferred to have your honorable consent and to crave your august presence."

"My Peach-blossom," he replied, "far be it from me to oppose what the heart of yourself and the honorable mother would receive. If it is a pleasure to you it is well. To me it is nothing. Do as you like about the matter; only do not expect me to follow, nor trouble me hereafter with frequent allusions to it. I shall be engaged in the weightier matters of looking after the elevation of the masses. Religion suits women and children, and so long as it is harmless, as yours seems to be, I shall not oppose it."

So saying he lit his pipe, and Toki retired with the tea tray.

* * * * * *

A little church of twelve native members had already been established within a few blocks of Matsuda's home. On the following Sunday three new members were baptized. They were the *Okkasan*, Toki and Kiku. Matsuda and the two older boys looked on at a respectful distance. The candidates all seemed overflowing with new-found joy, but only the younger boy, Saburo, seemed impressed by the sight. To Ichiro and his father it was rather a pretty superstition. It pleased the women and it was all right. They observed it with pretty much the same condescension that they showed when watching Shiro frolic on the floor at night as he played with his ball. Ichiro was a very bright boy, now fast approaching manhood. His whole attention, like that of his father, was to be given to "practical" matters.

CHAPTER XIV.

LIFE IN THE CAPITAL.

MATSUDA had shown himself an indispensable agent in the employment of the government, and so great was his zeal in wanting to do something for the elevation of the masses that he was employed again to act as general supervisor of some public works that were to be erected at various places throughout the interior. In order to do his work more thoroughly and to be accessible to his family at all times it became necessary for him to move them to Tokio. Here were good facilities for educating his children, and he placed the two boys, Ichiro and Saburo, in the Imperial University. The boys had the bright, quick minds for which their countrymen are noted, and learned eagerly all the branches that were taught at the time.

The family found that it was very pleasant living in Tokio. The city is simply a vast collection of parks and villages. The great castle was erected at first and then by degrees villages began to grow up around it until there was one hundred and twenty-five of them, with an aggregate population of more than a million. The parks are so numerous and extensive that many of the suburbs rather resemble encampments in the woods. There are fourteen hundred streets, all smooth and clean, though some of them are rather monotonous. Horses are rarely ever seen, so that the children play in the streets without danger of being run over by the *jinrikisha*.

The signs are interesting to one who has just learned their significance. Do you wish to find a drug store? Away down the street you will see a bag hanging out resembling the bag in which the

A Modern Improvement.

apothecary of Dai Nippon compounds his prescriptions. That is a drug store. A great cuttle fish signifies a kite store. *Sake* shops are conspicuous by their sign of a cypress trimmed into the shape of spheres. A large ball, one foot and a half in diameter, with a spike thrust through it, marks the confectioner's stand.

LIFE IN THE CAPITAL.

The castle rises up in the center of the city, surrounded by gloomy walls and broad deep moats of green water. In the Summer time these are covered with magnificent lotuses, and in the Winter with wild fowl. There are eleven miles of moats crossed by twenty-seven bridges that lead to gates in the tall and imposing ramparts. The stronghold of the Shoguns was well-nigh impregnable.

Within the walls are green swards, immense trees, and the ornamental houses of the nobility arranged in such an intricate labyrinth that a stranger wandering within would have a poor chance of finding his way out. Living in Tokio was more like old times at Osaka, for the city had not been so thoroughly Europeanized as Yokohama. Still to go in the business part and see the immense public works, banks and railway stations, one might imagine himself in Europe.

Here the ancient pastimes of native life were still in vogue. Kiku, though now a good-sized girl, had never lost her interest in the great day for girls, *Hina Matsuri*, often called by foreigners "The Feast of Dolls." This always comes on the third day of the third month, and is the jolliest day of all the year for the girls. Little images (we call them dolls) that have been stored up in the family for generations are brought out and exhibited, together with many new ones bought on that day. Shops are open and many things are sold on the day of the *Hina Matsuri* that are never sold at any other time. Hundreds of little maidens cluster around the doll stores reaching eagerly for their prizes and each trying to hand in her change at the same time and often for the same doll. The dolls are then gayly dressed by fond mothers, who devote the whole day to the girls and their frolics. The streets are crowded with chattering little maidens, their backs burdened with gayly appareled artificial babies. The doll vender is happy. He does a thriving business all day, selling more perhaps than he has sold in all the other days of the year together.

Dolls are everywhere. Rows of them are threaded on cords and wreathed in different designs for decorations. Every house or lawn has its little tea party, where many miniature tables are set, presided over by dolls and laid with doll tea sets.

This is a dreary, lonesome day for the boys, who mope through it in the best way they can, only sustained from utter dejection by the anticipation of the glorious "Fifth of the Fifth" (Fifth of May), when it will be their turn to transform earth into a boys' Paradise (Pandemonium for the sick neighbors). This is the Feast of Flags, in honor of Hachiman, god of war. Thousands of small boys fill the air with flying banners of every conceivable description, and blockade the streets as they gather in groups, spinning tops, riding wooden horses, forming processions of *daimyo*, and fighting the feudal wars over again in pantomime.

Before each boy's home is planted a tall bamboo, from the top of which dangles a huge paper carp fish. If there are several boys in the family each is represented by a fish flying and fluttering in the wind, exciting them to overcome all obstacles like the carp that leaps over waterfalls in his determined passage up stream.

The "Seventh of the Seventh" is also a great day with the boys. For on that day they can all go in swimming to their heart's content. On that day the evil sea monkey, that draws disobedient boys under the water when they run away and go in swimming without permission on other days, is chained, so they have nothing to fear, while papa or an older brother looks on at a safe distance to prevent accidents.

There are many games and other ways of amusement for the little ones in winter when they can not get out. At night they love to sit around the *hibachi* and listen to the *Obahsan* (grandmother) tell wonderful stories of feudal times. They also have many fairy stories and ghost stories. Rip Van Winkle is familiar to them in person if not in name. One form of the story as told by the grandmother in the softened glow of the *andon* to the eager listeners, represents a young man named Taro out fishing. A storm came up and he prayed loudly to the god of the sea. Presently there appeared on the crest of a wave the sea god, sitting on the back of a tortoise. Crying to Taro he said,

"Follow me and I will make you a happy man!"

Taro obeyed and leaped upon the back of the divine tortoise which immediately bore his burden away into a most wonderful land. The roads were lined with fragrant trees, and flowers were everywhere. Silvery lakes sparkled with the finest fish, and the trees were laden with ripe golden fruit. They passed through an imposing gateway and entered a gorgeous palace. Here trains of courtiers and beautiful maidens met him and bore him into the king's palace, and to a heavenly room where beautiful girls and bright-robed servants waited on him and did his every bidding. Life was a continual round of feasts by day and music by night. Many of the people had heads of gold, coral, and pearl, so common were these treasures.

After what he considered seven days of such unalloyed bliss, he remembered his poor father and mother at home, who needed his aid in supplying the fish for their daily food, or who were now mourning him lost in the storm. He secured permission from the king to return home for a few days and see to their wants. On his departure the king presented him with a box which he told him never to open under any circumstances. Then the tortoise bore him to the shore near his father's house, where he left him. Taro looked around, but could see nothing that looked familiar. He inquired of a gray-headed old fisherman for his father's hut. The old man told him that centuries ago there lived a family of that name, but now there was only their tombstone to tell that they had ever been. There was no trace of the house. Taro went to the graveyard in the valley, and by scraping the lichens from the stones found the graves of his parents. Then he felt sad, and yielded to a sudden desire to open the box. Immediately there flew out a purple vapor that enveloped him for a few moments. A cold shiver ran over him, his legs became stiff and bent, his face wrinkled, his teeth dropped out, and he was an old man four centuries a survivor of his generation. The weight of his age was too great to be borne, and he died the next day.

Another version that was of equal interest to the children, represented a pious woodcutter who found a fox in the woods and started to follow it. Soon he ran into an open space where a group of lovely girls sat playing checkers. Entranced by such a lovely sight in the midst of the forest, he stood still and gazed upon them for what seemed to him a few minutes. When he turned to move away his limbs felt stiff, and his ax handle crumbled to powder in his hand. Stooping to pick up the ax he found that his shaven face of the morning had grown a long gray beard reaching almost to his feet. He stumbled down the hill to the village and inquired for his home. All seemed new. Crowds of children flocked around him, and dogs barked at his heels, while older people shook their heads and marveled at such a sight as they had never seen before. He asked for his wife and children, but there were no such names known there, and the people thought him a lunatic. An old woman finally said that she was the seventh generation descended from the people he had mentioned. Whereupon the old man groaned in agony and returned to the woods, where he was never seen again.

Stories of great heroes like Yoshitsune are also very popular with the children, and at the same time instruct them in the history of their country.

In pleasant weather, which lasts a greater part of the year, the children play almost altogether out of doors. This open air freedom and the rigid etiquette in which they are drilled from babydom renders their intercourse singularly free from ill-mannered disputes and wrangles. But it is a mistake on the part of superficial writers to say that a Japanese child never fights, and that a baby is never known to cry. In the streets they are seen on their good behavior, but when confined together and placed under the same annoying circumstances as our children sometimes are, they as readily exhibit the effects of original sin. Yet, notwithstanding rare fits of naughtiness, common to all children, the "Wee Ones of Japan" have a jolly time, and are of but little trouble to their parents.

The festivities of Tokio and other cities were not confined to the children, for there are frequent occasions when older people have their "Great Days" too. One of the most popular of their festivals is the Chrysanthemum Exhibition. Every woman then has an opportunity to show herself an artist. The sacred flowers, in a rare state of perfection, due to long and patient cultivation, are brought and displayed in the most unimaginable ways. Houses and landscapes are made entirely of chrysanthemums. Then there are chrysanthemum streams, waterfalls and bridges crossed by chrysanthemum men and chrysanthemum horses, led by chrysanthemum bridles. All life seems to be reproduced in flowers that are still growing and gaining in brightness. The forms of the various objects are made of woven wire, through the intestices of which the living plants are woven, and then the interior is filled with moist earth.

The Empress took great interest in these exhibits, and did much to advance their success. Much credit is also due to this most excellent lady for her cooperation in many things that added to the pleasure and welfare of her subjects. She often visited the sick in person and ministered to their sufferings in a modest way that won their regard and sincere affection.

CHAPTER XV.

ELEVATING THE MASSES.

MATSUDA had been commissioned to use all available foreign helps and suggestions in the prosecution of the government work in the interior. His chief work at first lay in founding schools and erecting school buildings. Many others were commissioned with the same work, and within a few years there was scarcely a hamlet that did not have its neat little government schoolhouse, constructed according to the latest designs, and furnished with patent folding desks, blackboards, charts and other modern conveniences. It was a pleasant sight to a foreign traveler to see these filled with bright-eyed children and to hear their sprightly answers in recitation.

But improvements did not stop here. One good thing led to another. Government engineers came along and constructed roads through the hills and erected bridges over hitherto impassable streams. Within a few years the whole face of the country was changed. European hotels sprang up along the highways and in all the towns and villages of any importance. The postal service was perfected still more, modeled after that of the United States, and telegraph offices were to be found in some of the most remote places. Crime was suppressed by prompt execution of the laws. Well ventilated and scrupulously clean prisons were erected. The prisoners were not allowed to languish inside the walls during the day and plot new mischief, but were put out to work, where, by honest labor under God s pure open sky, they might improve both body and mind. They were also in better frame of mind to consider moral and religious subjects. Mr. Neesima, afterwards founder of the Doshisha University, once gave a copy of the New Testament to a prison official, who in turn gave it to a well-educated prisoner convicted of manslaughter. The latter became interested in the "New Way," and taught it to his fellow prisoners. Afterwards a fire broke out that consumed the building. When the doors were opened the prisoners, instead of escaping, as they could have done, remained to help extinguish the flames, then returned to their work as usual. This caused great surprise, for such a thing had never been heard of before. When it was learned that it was on account of the teachings of the New Testament by the scholar, he was at once pardoned and set at liberty. He did not leave, however, but remained to teach the "New Way" to others.

No little of the material prosperity, as well as moral improvement, was due to faithful Christian teachers in the employment of the government. They founded a system of scientific education in many communities, and planted Christian churches, so that many were both enlightened intellectually, and turned unto the Lord in their hearts.

Missionaries of all denominations now went by permission of the government into all parts of the land, and established schools and churches in every province, till it seemed to the sanguine workers that a complete conquest of the country for Christ was not far off. Native converts showed themselves enthusiastic and able workers. One peculiar feature of the work soon became apparent, something that has never been known before in any mission field of the world. Most of the converts were men, and largely from the more intelligent classes. Forty per cent of the native Christians to-day are from the *samurai* classes. These have always favored western ideas, while the masses of the people are still conservative, many of them opposed to foreign civilization so suddenly thrust upon them, and still devout adherents of the old religions. The failure of the women to be converted is largely due to their inaccessibility. They are not allowed to attend places where large crowds are congregated, and can only be reached by the female workers going to their homes.

One great need soon became apparent. The evangelistic work must be done mainly by natives, for many of the people in the interior did not understand the foreigner, and a few still hated him as "the foreign devil," and would not listen to a missionary, at least, not with the same degree of attention and earnestness that they showed to one of their own nation who had passed from darkness unto light, and who could tell better than any one else the effects of religion in his own soul. But mere conversion was not sufficient training for those who had knotty questions to answer before intelligent audiences, so the native preachers soon began with their quick minds to evolve a system of theology out of their former Buddhistic subsoil, with results that were not always in accordance with orthodoxy. It was necessary for them to be more thoroughly and accurately instructed, but it was almost impossible to do it at home. Some who could afford it attended the great universities in Europe and America, but there were many zealous workers who could not undertake such an expensive course. Theological departments were added to the Christian schools in order to supply this lack as far as possible, but still better equipped institutions are needed for the training of native workers. Many of the Christian schools can not obtain orthodox teachers, but have to take those that are trained in the government schools, many of which are skeptical. The brightest of the Japanese have seen the folly of Shinto and Buddhism, and therefore conclude that all religion is but superstition, which must vanish before the light of scientific education.

There were many others who cared nothing for any religion, but, seeing the results of Christianity, were in favor of making it the State Religion as a matter of policy. Thousands stood ready to enter the churches if they could only be allowed to "adopt" Christianity, and put it on in outward form as they had done Romanism in the Sixteenth Century. The great trouble always has been to reach the *hearts* and *consciences* of those who have been trained under

Buddhism and Confucianism, and who are just breaking away from the old paths. Some missionaries have thought that it might be a good policy to compromise and leave off some of our most objectionable dogmas. Hence they have preached an uninspired Gospel of a Christ who was not divine. But they made a fatal mistake. Only an infallible Bible and a Divine Saviour, who is also a Judge, can break those rationalistic hearts and satisfy those craving minds. If we are simply to preach morals, they have a code of morals already that would condemn the best of us. If we simply proclaim a great human teacher, they follow one who existed before ours, and whose adherents number one-third of the population of the world.

Medical Missions at first were a great factor for good in Japan. A physician can reach many whom a preacher could never approach. The skill and tender regard of the Christian doctors aided many to understand in a realistic sense the love and compassion of the Great Physician. Native physicians have now become proficient and have taken the place of foreign skill, which is well. Japan has too much national pride and independence of spirit to rely longer than is necessary upon others for help.

Foreign teachers were also dispensed with as native scholars became competent to take up their work and complete it. The sons of the nobility who attended the great foreign universities stood at the head with the brightest of American and European intellects, sometimes surpassing them in special branches, such as the difficult and ancient Oriental languages. The metaphysical abstractions of Herbert Spencer and the vague theories of German rationalists, so difficult and dry to our students, were greedily learned and adopted by them. Such things alone seemed sufficiently weighty to satisfy, for a while at least, the abnormal cravings of intellects naturally bright, but for ages imprisoned.

At Kioto in 1875 was founded by Mr. Neesima the Doshisha College, destined to do a great work in the enlightenment of the native youth. Joseph Hardy Neesima is a central figure in the history of Japanese Christianity. He was ten years old when Perry landed, and at a very early age became interested in the advancement of his country. He gave up Shinto when a boy, and seeing in a Chinese tract the words, "In the beginning God created the heavens and the earth," he said, "That is the God I am seeking." He escaped from Japan and found his way to America, where he became converted, and received a thorough theological education. He was afterwards pardoned by the government for leaving the country, an offense punishable with death, and burning with zeal, he returned to Kioto. where in 1875 he founded Doshisha College. In 1886 he enlarged the college to the rank of a University, letting it be known that he intended it to be strictly a Christian institution. With this understanding he received from Japanese statesmen $60,000, and from an American gentleman $100,000. In 1889 Amherst College honored him with the degree of LL.D. His school grew from the beginning, having a large per cent. of its students preparing for missionary work. There are often one hundred conversions a year among the students. It is missionary in the truest sense of the word. Japanese Christians owe much to this able and wise man. He died in 1890, mourned by all classes. A special tabernacle had to be erected to hold the thousands who attended his funeral. A large banner was borne by friends from Tokio inscribed with his own words, "FREE EDUCATION AND SELF-GOVERNING CHURCHES, IF THESE GO TOGETHER THE COUNTRY WILL STAND FOR ALL GENERATIONS." Another banner was inscribed, "FROM THE BUDDHISTS OF OSAKA."

CHAPTER XVI.

OFF FOR HARVARD.

ICHIRO applied himself so diligently that he completed the course at the University in an incredibly short time. It was now his great ambition to go to America and attend Harvard for a special course as so many of his acquaintances were doing. This would involve heavy expense, and it did not seem possible for his father to send him. Matsuda's salary, though liberal, had barely supported his family, and he saw no way of adding enough to his income to risk such a venture. It was a great disappointment to him and to the whole family, for Ichiro had shown real brilliancy of intellect, and only lacked thorough training to become one of the lights of the Empire. During the summer he accompanied his father on a tour of the interior preparatory to learning something of the government work so that he might secure a position as engineer. While they were gone the rest of the family got together and planned a loving conspiracy. None of them were willing for Ichiro to fail in his heart's desire for a thorough education, so they planned how they might send him. Grandmother, though now old and, as she thought, useless, still had a quick mind. She proposed to show Kiku how to do the housekeeping and thus allow Toki to give more of her time to literature and art. Toki had recently been contributing articles to a leading journal in Tokio, and had just received a flattering offer for others at a good price. She was also expert with the brush, and had illustrated several articles. By this way she recognized that she could add considerably to the family income. Saburo now spoke up and said that he had been offered a position as tutor to some classes in the University which would pay for his own tuition. He had not accepted because it would cause him to have to remain a year or two longer.

"However," he said, "if by doing so I can help brother I am more than willing, and will accept the offer in the morning."

"There's my good boy!" exclaimed his mother. "You shall never lose by your generosity."

When Ichiro returned his mother related to him and his father, as they sat at tea, what had been done. He was almost overcome with delight, and was so profuse in his thanks that they could never regret having undertaken so much for him. Matsuda at first seemed skeptical as to the practicability of the scheme, but they won him over and the arrangements began to be made.

It should have been mentioned that before this time Ichiro had become altogether too important a character to be known simply as "Number One," as his name signified, and he was given a new name according to the prevailing custom. Some young men formerly changed their names several times, but the law now forbids so many changes. Ichiro became

Jiro (Jeé-ro), and as such we shall henceforth know him. As for Saburo, he was still content to be known as "Number Three."

All was now bustle and activity in the family. Jiro must have American clothes, and trunks and valises to pack them in. Mrs. Green, the wife of the pastor, to whose church the women of the family now belonged, was of great assistance in suggesting what would be necessary, and assisting in the preparations. She herself had come from New England, and had so many things to tell about Boston and Cambridge that the family almost felt that they were acquainted with the people with whom Jiro would be associated.

Jiro himself practiced eating with a knife and fork instead of the national chopsticks. He had become somewhat accustomed to American food at the hotels, and spoke the English language fluently. So he would neither suffer embarrassment on account of a lack of knowledge on those points nor be subject to delay in his studies while learning such things.

At last the day of his departure arrived. After separating from the family amid many tears and prayers for his welfare, he took the train for Yokohama, where he found the great floating city, capable of transporting twelve hundred persons, ready at the wharf to bear him away to that distant land whence the immortal Perry had come with his wonderful fleet, and which is the El Dorado of every Japanese boy's dreams. It was with a beating heart that he mounted the deck and prepared to look for the last time for several years upon his native land, still "The Land of the Sunrise." A few years ago such a trip was forbidden on penalty of death. Now any one was allowed to go to America if he was only able to do so. There were several of his acquaintances on board, some for Harvard and some for Yale. So they had a pleasant time during the two weeks' voyage.

Two weeks after Jiro sailed Toki received a card written in mid-ocean and mailed on a passing steamer, signifying that he was safe and well so far. Two weeks more and another announced his safe arrival in San Francisco, and promised a long letter so soon as he should become settled at College and acquainted with his surroundings.

From time to time the family heard of his gratifying progress and felt more than repaid for all that they had sacrificed for him. He often wrote about the strange customs that he saw. He said that he had been with some of the students to call on some young ladies, a thing that seems an impossibility to a Japanese mind. A few visits to such charming creatures, however, removed his scruples and he learned to enjoy their society. It still seemed strange to him, though, that young people could marry against their parents' will. Yet young Japan is fast learning, and there is no telling what Jiro himself will do some day.

It had been Toki's one prayer in sending Jiro abroad that in Christian America he might see the power of Christianity in its effects upon the people and become so influenced by it that he would be led to embrace it. She did not realize that America was different from Japan, not having one or two religions to which everybody must belong, but a country where all religions are taught, and where many have no religion at all. Judge of her bitter disappointment when she read the following paragraph in one of Jiro's letters:

"America is not so much Christian after all. There seems to me to be as much wickedness here as in Japan. Very few people, except preachers, women and children, pay much attention to religion. Sunday is not kept as strictly as it is in Japan. Trains, street cars and saloons do their greatest business on Sunday. Monday morning papers are full of accounts of crimes committed by drunken men who were idle on Sunday and have nothing to do but beat their wives and fight over the gambling tables. I also find that the people that are religious worship many gods. I have been to several churches of different denominations as a matter of curiosity, and each denounces all the others. If they worshiped the same God it would not be so. I care not to disturb your faith, but this thing called religion seems to me to be a poor thing as compared with intellectual pursuits."

This wrankled like a poisoned arrow in the heart of the devoted mother. After all her planning, when she honestly thought in the fear of God that she was doing the best for her boy, it now seemed that she could not have made a greater mistake. She concealed that part of the letter from the rest of the family and carried her distress to Mrs. Green, who had so often helped and comforted her before.

"Ah," said the good woman when she had read the letter, "he is looking at things altogether from his own standpoint. Many of the things he speaks of are, in a sense, true, but Christianity is not responsible for them. There are many wicked people in America who come from all parts of the world. Jiro has not yet considered the other side. There has been much done by Christians that he must acknowledge has been of untold benefit to the world. He is bright and will come all right yet. This is only a superficial observation. Pray for him and trust God to do what is best."

An hour's conversation with this consecrated and sensible woman reassured the anxious mother, and she returned home with a lighter heart, though still serious. She kept her thoughts to herself. She did not wish to distress the others who had so lovingly entered into her plans. Perhaps all would come right yet. It was not worth while to mention the matter to Matsuda, for he saw things as Jiro did, and could not have offered any sympathy or showed any concern. He rejoiced to learn that his son was standing on equal footing with the brightest students in America who were with him in college, and that was all he cared about, provided, of course, that Jiro did not fall into vicious habits. He wanted both his morals and his manners to be perfect, and cautioned him on that subject whenever he wrote. Matsuda's sole concern was for the Emperor and the intellectual elevation of his people.

CHAPTER XVII.

AFTER FOUR YEARS.

TIME has made its changes in the family we left at Tokio. The aged grandmother has been laid to rest; not the rest of Nirvana for which she once longed, but the sleep in Jesus from which she will awake to behold the righteousness of her Lord and dwell forever with God and his saints. Bro. Green conducted the funeral, and prayed that her son and grandson might follow her example. Matsuda was visibly affected, but as yet he did not realize his need and the power of the Gospel. He was a man of affairs.

Saburo is now associate editor of a large daily paper and an active worker in the church and the missions of the capital.

Shiro is almost grown, well advanced in his classes, and a devout Christian worker. It is his great aim to be a minister of the Gospel. He sees the need of his countrymen and longs to do something for them. They are grasping, like his own father, for the results of Christianity without first becoming possessed of the power that it gives to elevate and reform mankind. He yearns for a thorough education to fit him for his great life work. But the resources of the family have been exhausted in supporting Jiro in America, so that he can not hope to go there himself for many years.

He has very often thought that if some wealthy generous-minded American knew how he longed for an education he would open the way. There must be an abundance of everything in America. He had just read that the cost of firing one of their great guns *one time would support two missionaries in Japan for a whole year.*

Kiku is now an accomplished young lady and as well deserving the name of the royal flower, "Chrysanthemum," as when her mother gave it to her in infancy. She has the beauty of her mother's youth with the added charm of Christian graces. She is active in every good work, full of love for her country, and has before her the prospect of great usefulness.

As for Toki, time has left its mark on her face also, but has not destroyed its attractiveness. She is counting the days till the great ship shall land bringing her boy again to her arms. How have the four years affected him? Will he be a nobler, better son? Will he be more susceptible to religious influence, or further away from it? Such thoughts as these daily arose in her head, and she prayed that he might soon be led to Christ.

At last the welcome day arrived, and with it came Jiro. He wore a nobby suit of American clothes, a curled American mustache, twirled a cane, and bore himself with a free American air. He had not fully outgrown the national etiquette and inborn respect for his parents, but outwardly showed them polite attention and seemed sincerely glad to be back in his own beautiful country and happy home. How handsome and attractive he looked, and how proud they all were of him! He gave interesting accounts of his

Kiku.
(Chrysanthemum.)

voyage and discussed intelligently the people and countries that he had seen.

Within a few days, however, his generous younger

brothers found that a wall had grown up between them and him. He was removed into an entirely different sphere. Henceforth they could never be affectionate brothers again. They must now follow different channels of life. In the new, varied and rushing Japan this is not hard to do; but the hardest thing for them was to have sacrificed the best part of youth for him, and to have received no better return. Their brother no longer cared for them. Kiku tried to enlist him in some religious reading one day, but he replied by quoting a whole page from Herbert Spencer that frightened her by its meaningless jargon.

"That is my religion," he said. "In spiritual matters wise men are agnostics."

The gentle girl, who knew nothing of what he had written to her mother on a former occasion, was stunned by surprise and inexpressible grief. When she related this interview to her mother the latter was also distressed, but wisely answered,

"My dear, I feel that we have done what was best as far as we could judge. Why it all has resulted so I can not say. We must try to show to your brother by Christian example and loving lives that religion is better than philosophy. With God's help we may at last lead him to see the better way. Would that your father had set him a Christian example."

Matsuda, however, was thoroughly pleased with his son's advancement, and with his superiority to the notions of women and children. He lost no time in securing for him a government position of good salary and light work so that he could continue intellectual pursuits.

* * * * * *

Shortly after this Matsuda was in a railway wreck in which he received a broken leg. It was in the hot season and complications set up that confined him to his bed for several months. Dr. Green, who was also a skilled surgeon, treated him and won his regard, both by his wonderful skill and by his disinterested kindness. Matsuda often wondered at receiving so much sincere attention, when the bill for services was only nominal. It certainly was not for money. The Doctor often sat with him after his professional duties were over, engaging him in intelligent conversation and trying to cheer him, since he felt despondent at losing so much time. Finally, one day, Matsuda asked,

"Doctor, why is it that you show so much interest in me when I have never done anything for you, not even attending your church?"

"I am only trying to follow my Master," replied the good man. "He, the Great Physician, loved and served even his worst enemies. I wish you would read his life in the New Testament and become convinced that He is what you need." The Doctor was glad of this opportunity to speak a word without intruding, knowing his patient's feelings before in regard to religion. Matsuda felt that it would be politeness to accept his suggestion, besides, he had some little curiosity to see the insignificant little book that had seemed such a comfort to his mother and wife. During his sickness he had noticed, as never before, the difference between his own Christian family and those of many of his acquaintances with whom he had stopped. His duties for the past few years had not allowed him to be at home much, and he had not fully appreciated the comfort and peace of a Christian life. He thought over it after the Doctor had gone. Perhaps, after all, Christianity had benefited his home. When his wife came in he delighted her by saying:

"Toki, I wish you would bring me the Testament that seems to be so entertaining to you. I thought I would read a little, as I can do nothing else."

"With the greatest pleasure, honored husband," she replied. "I have often wished that I might ask you to read it, but you made me promise not to press you in the matter of religion."

She brought it to him and then went out with a prayer in her heart that God might lead him to the light. If only Jiro would read it too!

That night when Matsuda read the evening paper he was greatly impressed by a sensible article from his own son, Saburo, entitled, "Christ, the Hope of Japan." Day by day he read the New Testament with increasing interest. The family could see that he was attracted, and wisely forbore to mention the matter till he had formed his own conclusions. When the good Doctor came in a few days after he found his patient filled with enthusiasm.

"*Eureka!*" Matsuda exclaimed. "What a fool I have been. Giving my best time and energies to the elevation of my people, depending on my personal theories, when here is the problem solved. Henceforth I am a Christian. Such wonderful wisdom, such a beneficent spirit! Confucius and Buddha are nowhere. Doctor, why has not this been adopted by every government and practiced by every nation?"

"Ah," replied the Doctor, "all have not heard, and then the carnal heart does not receive the things of the Gospel. I am rejoiced to know that the Lord has revealed himself to you."

It was amid general rejoicing that the family learned of Matsuda's decision, and the only thought now was, How would it affect Jiro? When the young man returned that evening he went as usual to his father's room, and kneeling by his couch saluted him and inquired about his health.

"I am happy to say that I am improving rapidly," replied Matsuda. "Thanks to the patient care of your mother and sister, and the skillful treatment of the good Doctor."

"I am happy to hear you speak so," said Jiro. "Great Japan can ill afford to spare for so long a time the services of such an important officer as you have shown yourself."

Then noticing the New Testament at his father's side, he looked surprised and said:

"Can it be possible that sickness has so oppressed my princely father that he can find entertainment in the book of the hated Yasu religion?"

"Indeed," replied Matsuda. "I have found this little book most helpful and instructive. I firmly believe that it contains the principles which alone can make of Japan a great nation like her western neighbors. I only regret that I have not learned it sooner. I mean to advocate Christianity from now henceforth. I wish you, too, my son, would read the little book and at least examine into the matter."

A look of surprised pity overspread the fine features of the young man as his father spoke. He replied with a polite smile scarcely concealing contempt,

"The honored father has a right to do as he pleases. If you prefer this new religion to those which are older and well tried it is well. There is nothing in any of them to satisfy an ambitious nature. Science is the highest form of religion. Only Metaphysics can furnish food for the highest intellects, such as Japan is now producing. I beg pardon for differing, but I think you have made a mistake. Japan can never be reached in that way. She has passed beyond the stage of superstition and fable."

Toki and Kiku now appeared with the tea, and Matsuda, seeing that it was useless to reason the subject, and not wishing to distress them, allowed it to drop for the time.

CHAPTER XVIII.

A NEW MOVEMENT OF THE YOUNG PEOPLE.

AFTER tea Jiro lit a cigarette and strolled across the park to a favorite tea garden where he was in the habit of spending his evenings in company with a number of his friends and former schoolmates, some of whom had been to Harvard and Yale.

Pretty black-eyed girls brought in tiny cups of straw-colored tea on little lacquer tables, then prepared the room for the usual entertainment. The twang of the *samisen* (guitar) could be heard already in an adjoining room accompanied by soft mouse-like voices. Soon the *shoji* were drawn back and a group of *geisha* entered and arranged themselves on the mats. They were elegantly dressed, sweet-faced little creatures whose sole business was to entertain, and usually to corrupt young men. One played the *samisen* while the others went through various motions called dancing though they did not use their feet. The young men sat, alternately smoking, eating bonbons and drinking tea, while they watched in a listless manner the gay little creatures wearing themselves out in their efforts to please.

Girl and Samisen.

After that they strolled out through

the lovely gardens lighted by hundreds of many-colored paper lanterns, and in hearing of the sounds of revelry from the various houses around them. There, at mid-night, amid such surroundings, and after such an evening's preparation, they formed plans for the elevation (?) of their country. They had often spoken together about the alarming tendencies of the people to become enthralled again by Buddhism, or, what was worse, the Yasu religion, and now they felt that something must be done at once. Jiro was the first to speak.

"Boys," said he, "you all know how I stand on this great question of our country's elevation. I believe that only mental enlightenment and material improvements can accomplish the work. Hitherto I have not thought it advisable to push the matter, but to-night I have learned astonishing news that prompts me to urge immediate action. My father, whom we all considered proof against all such superstition, has actually adopted the hated Jesus Doctrine."

"*Naruhodo!*" exclaimed the others in one breath.

"Yes," continued Jiro, "he proposes to give his whole time to the work of spreading abroad a religion such as plunged our country into such a state of disorder over two hundred years ago, and from which she has never recovered. I feel that when such men as he are being seduced by it that it is time for those who have the welfare of the country at heart, to act, and that in a decided way."

"Ditto!" exclaimed Ichitaro, one of his chums. "You have struck it right. We must do something.

I see from to-day's paper that the Buddhists are also making a last determined effort to enslave us. They have now over fifty thousand priests, and are building a temple to cost eleven million dollars, all of which must come from the pockets of people too poor to eat the very rice that they raise. Some of the Buddhists are also adopting Christian methods. such as Sunday-schools, preaching, circulating literature, holding prayer-meetings; and one sect has gone so far in imitation of our common enemy as to proclaim salvation through simple faith in Amida Butsu, whatever they may mean by such an abstraction. Anything to keep the people duped and under the power of the priests and preachers! Something must be done."

"Well, what shall it be?" inquired a third.

"I move," said Jiro, "that we here and now organize a society for the diffusing of scientific knowledge. We will have nothing special to say against any religion, since that would only fan the flame of fanaticism, but the diffusing of knowledge will stop them all."

Priest and Assistant.

"I second the motion!" exclaimed Ichitaro.

Thus out there under the cryptomeria trees at midnight these young patriots (?) established an institution called the S. S. S. (Spencerean Scientific Society). Jiro was made President and Ichitaro Secretary. By the next night they had secured a place of meeting, and twenty new members were enrolled. None were eligible to membership except men of the highest literary and scientific attainments, but, to show how plentiful these were by now, the Society had a hundred members by the end of the month. Several young men from Yokohama came up on the train once a week to the weekly public exercises. They now owned a magnificent club-room, and had engaged a number of *geisha* to play for their special entertainment between the reading of the learned essays. A monthly magazine was published called "The Spencerean Review," which contained the best essays of the Society and the results of the latest scientific investigation. In this way they did a good work in developing the minds of the people at large, though nothing was said about God nor religion of any kind. Such things were beneath notice.

To the tears of his sister and mother and the entreaties of his father and brothers Jiro was equally deaf. He knew they meant well, and he loved them, but they could not understand his great work, so that it was useless to reason with him. He was at home very little now. He came in from the office at night, and as soon as he had tea he went to the club rooms.

The following paragraph in the Spencerean Review came like an earthquake shock to the anxious family who had never received any intimation of such a thing, and which they could scarcely believe possible after what Jiro had written once before:

"We are happy to announce the marriage in September of our popular and learned President, Mr. Jiro Kimura, to Miss Jeanette Anderson, of Boston, Mass., U. S. A. It is now not an uncommon thing for intelligent young American and English ladies to marry Japanese noblemen. We trust that this union may be a happy one, and that it may add to the usefulness of our already efficient friend."

"Alas!" thought the aggrieved parents, "in some respects our country is growing too fast. We never thought it possible that it could come to this." Even then as they looked across the street they saw a girl in hybrid costume of both native and foreign style, actually leaning over the gate simpering, chewing gum, and *talking with a young man!* It was well for Grandmother Kimura that she was at rest, for she could never have survived such a shock as this. Again Toki went to Mrs. Green for comfort and advice.

"This is indeed a serious case," said the good woman. "But we must try to make the best of it. It may be God's way of bringing your gifted son to see the true way. It is to be hoped that the young lady is a true Christian woman and not a mere adventuress. If she comes with the right motive she will be of great assistance in our work. If not, we must hope and pray for the best. Look on the bright side. I have been a follower of the Lord longer than you have, and I know 'He doeth all things well.'"

Thus reassured Toki made no remonstrances, and there was no family "scene," as Jiro naturally expected there would be. He was surprised at the spirit with which they all entered into the preparations for the event. His mother and sister packed his valise and dismissed him with their prayers when he started again on his journey across the waters. His father had also become reconciled, and bade him good-bye as affectionately as before. Then they all waited, hoping and praying that good might come of it all.

CHAPTER XIX.

THE LIGHT GROWS BRIGHTER.

TOKI had one happy event to look forward to during Jiro's absence, and that was her husband's baptism. For she had no doubt that as soon as he was able he would join the church and be baptized. But it seemed that he had no such intentions, for as soon as he was able to travel he arranged for a tour through the districts where he had labored as government agent. He would carry a supply of Testaments, employ colporteurs and endeavor to introduce the study of the Bible into the schools as the best means of making good citizens. Before he left, Toki ventured to inquire if he did not intend to join the church. But he replied that he would not wait for that now. He was anxious to get to see the school authorities before the next term opened, and to employ a large number of agents to carry out the work of distributing Bibles in the rural districts. He did not feel that it was necessary to join the church; he might have a wider influence if he did not. At some other time he might.

These and other remarks led Toki to fear that he had never been converted. She feared that he was grasping after the husk, while failing to secure the kernel of Christianity, a tendency then and now prevalent in Japan.

Before his departure Matsuda busied himself visiting the various government officials and consulting with them about his proposed plan. He was anxious to get Christianity adopted at once as the State Religion. Count Ito, the Prime Minister, was highly pleased with the idea, and promised to do all in his power to bring his plans to perfection. The matter of adopting Christianity as a State Religion now became a subject of discussion. But as soon as the papers published the fact that such a thing was anticipated there was a general protest from the missionaries, the very ones of all others from whom Matsuda expected support. He had gone to Kioto to place Shiro in the Doshisha,* and was there when he heard of the opposition of the missionaries. In great surprise he inquired of Mr. Neesima why it was that they did not favor it. That godly man replied,

"The Christian religion is not a mere form or a code like Buddhism or Shinto. It is not a matter of legislation, but is to be secured only by personal repentance and faith. A new birth is necessary, and that comes not by any sovereign's order, but through the Holy Spirit. The Christian religion can not be 'adopted,' it is in the heart. Thus you see why it is that the missionaries oppose what could be only a form and what might take the place of vital union with Christ, the Head of the Church."

Matsuda pondered over these things as he went about his work. In the meanwhile he distributed many Bibles and tracts, and induced hundreds to look

---

*This was before Mr. Neesima's death.

with greater favor upon Christianity. Still he felt a misgiving lest he had made a mistake. Had he that "new heart?" He had no evidence of it. He felt that he had simply put on Christianity, and that not from any personal need, but because he thought it a good means of accomplishing his designs in enlightening his countrymen so that they might compare favorably with other nations. He had not thought of any life to come, nor of their need of a spiritual preparation for it. He now felt himself a lost man and a hypocrite. So strong did the feeling grow upon him that he had to give up his work and return home, where he greatly distressed his wife on telling her of his condition. Dr. Green was sent for, and immediately told her that she should rejoice that her husband had been shown his error. "Would," he said, "that many others now under a similar delusion might see their condition!"

He found Matsuda a sincere penitent, and opened up the way of life to him in such a plain, simple manner that by the help of God he was enabled to trust in a crucified Saviour and not in his own schemes for salvation.

On the following Sunday there was an unusually large attendance at church to hear Matsuda's experience and to see him baptized, for he was now well known to the whole country. When he next entered the field it was as an evangelist. The power of the Most High was with him and hundreds were annually led to Christ through his preaching.

* * * * * *

Three months after his departure Jiro returned with his bride. To the delight of the family she was a sweet, sensible young woman, and a devout Christian. Jiro paid her great respect, as is the custom of Japanese toward foreign ladies, or even their wives when in foreign dress. He spent more of his evenings at home now, and when he went out she went with him. He refrained from attacking Christianity for fear it would offend her, and he frequently accompanied her to church. He remained a member of the S. S. S., but not with such a decided motive as at first. Jeannette dealt prudently and lovingly with him, and it was confidently hoped by the family that she might yet influence him to become a Christian, since he was now the only one of the family who was not a worker for Christ. But he belonged to the intellectual Aristocracy, and it required time and the Holy Spirit to bring him over. He received a good salary, and generously promised to send Shiro to America to finish his theological education.

CHAPTER XX.

OUTLOOK BEFORE THE WAR.

THINGS moved along quietly with our friends till the Summer of 1894. A Parliament had been established, but on account of disagreements among rival parties it was dissolved by the Emperor. There were still some ultra-conservative leaders who favored restricting the privileges of foreign residents, while many wanted to open the entire country to those who wished to settle in the interior. At the beginning of Japan's connection with other nations, not being skilled in diplomacy, she had been imposed upon by unfavorable treaties. She was allowed only 5 per cent. tariff, and had no jurisdiction over foreigners, who were to be responsible to their respective consuls instead. Her crude laws at the time justified this, but by now she had adopted civilized legislation, and demanded recognition among civilized nations. In order to induce foreign countries to consent to a revision of the treaties, the Japanese began to require strict adherence to their side of the contract, which forbade any foreigner traveling in the interior without a passport, or from residing anywhere outside of the few treaty-ports. This threatened great embarrassment to the missionaries who were located from one end of the country to the other, and they began using their influence to secure treaty revision. We are happy to say that during the year 1894 a satisfactory revision was secured to the treaties relating to England and the United States, thus opening the way for other nations to follow suit.

To no one did this bring more happiness than to Matsuda. He both felt it due to his country, and especially desired it on account of the greater freedom it would secure to missionary workers. This year was one of great prosperity. Education was greatly advanced by the twenty-nine thousand elementary schools, the fifty schools of middle class, the more than forty normal schools, besides ten universities, one law school and ten law colleges, in all of which, taken together, were nearly four million pupils, with an annual cost to the Government of more than eight million dollars.

Travel and communication were also greatly advanced by the two thousand miles of railway, ten thousand miles of telephone and twenty thousand miles of telegraph. There were now fifty thousand miles of postal roads; and one hundred and fifty million pieces of mail going through the domestic mails annually, to say nothing of the million pieces that went to foreign countries. Out of more than seven hundred and twenty-five newspapers and magazines, one hundred and twenty were published in Tokio alone. The *Morning News* of Tokio has a daily circulation of 100,000, and a paper of the same name in Osaka, 130,000 per day, yet there is not a Sunday paper in all Japan! Religious journals were increasing, the number then being about seventy. Over twenty thousand books were published in the preceding year, a large part of them being by native authors. The Yokohama Bible House, through Matsuda and his workers, had sold during the year nearly five thousand Bibles, besides more than thirty thousand Testaments and portions of Testaments. Libraries were in all large cities, the one at the Imperial University at Tokio having 80,000 volumes in European languages alone. It was by this time a well known fact, in which all took commendable pride, that in Japan a greater proportion of the people could read and write than in any other country in the world. What a change in thirty years!

Christianity was now an acknowledged factor in the new civilization. There were in Tokio one hundred Protestant churches, and nearly three hundred more in the Empire, seventy-eight of which were self-supporting. Presbyterians led in strength among Protestants, though the Congregationalists were also very strong. In May, 1894, the Bible School at Yokohama, under the control of the Baptists, was converted into a full-fledged Theological Seminary, with prospects of being highly useful in training men for the work. The *Japan Mail* estimated the number of Christians at one hundred thousand, over half of whom were Greek and Roman Catholic. Among the more than 80,000 physicians a "Christian Doctors' Society" had been formed for the purpose of placing the Bible in the hands of every physician in the Empire. The Chief Justice of the Supreme Court was a Christian and President of the local Y. M. C. A.

Y. M. C. A. Hall, Tokio.

In the first Diet twelve members and the Speaker were Christians, and two Christians held high office by the direct appointment of the Emperor. Thus it seems that the Christians formed a class that was not to be despised.

Yet there are twice as many lepers as Christians in Japan!

Shinto and Buddhism are in their death struggles, but the last struggles are hard ones. A desperate effort is being made to overthrow the new religion by adopting its methods. The Buddhist priests alone number 52,794; more than all Protestant Christians combined. They also have nearly one hundred thousand temples, some of which are supported by public money, though mainly to preserve them as relics for sight-seers to look at. Shinto, the State Religion, has 191,968 temples and shrines, and nearly fifteen thousand priests.

Notwithstanding the fact that everything was progressing so favorably with the nation at home, and with its foreign relations in general, it was plain to those who read the signs of the times that a storm was soon to burst forth. While many dreaded it, yet the nation as a whole was anxious to see it past. Conservative China in her haughty arrogance had long despised these enterprising "Yankees of the East," and lost no opportunity of showing her spite. Time and again, for years past, insults had been borne by the Japanese, till it was fast coming to a point when forbearance would cease to be a virtue.

The peninsula of Corea, though joining China, and

under the suzerainty of the latter, was a place of great mercantile importance to Japan, and many Japanese citizens lived there. There were many ultra-conservatives in Corea, and a few Japanese soldiers were needed to protect their countrymen. These were frequently interfered with by the Chinese, and several difficulties finally resulted in an examination by both powers, and the formation of a treaty, under which neither party was to send troops into the peninsula without the consent of the other, though a necessary force was allowed to remain for protection of traders.

Having herself tasted of the good things of modern civilization, Japan possessed the *Altruistic* spirit that led her to desire to introduce the same advantages among her benighted neighbors on the Continent. China was mighty in extent, old in her customs, and very proud in her manners, so that nothing could be accomplished there. Corea was nearer, and though very old and non-progressive herself, was yet a dependent country in regard to China, and under many obligations to Japan. The Japanese Minister in Corea had great influence with the King, to whom he gave many helpful suggestions as to modern progress. To the credit of the King, let it be said that he entered heartily into many of the reforms suggested by the Japanese. China beheld this with much jealousy, and through her Minister succeeded in arousing much opposition. The country became divided into two parties, the Progressionists, siding with the King, and the Conservatives, siding with China. The

King continued to follow the advice of Japan and to carry out many needed reforms in the government and in the army, besides sending a number of intelligent young men to Japan to learn the new way.

The Conservative element became more and more turbulent, and finally in the spring of 1894 they formed a mob and stormed the King's palace. China received news of the outbreak and immediately despatched two large armies to the peninsula, one by land, the other by sea, with the ostensible purpose of protecting the King, but really in order to defeat his progressive measures. The presence of this army was a great menace to Japan and a violation of the treaty made not long before with Li Hung Chang, viceroy of China. Japan had not ventured to send an army in addition to her troops already quartered there, though she had suffered many indignities. Even after the restoration of comparative quiet, China showed no disposition to recall her forces, and the situation was becoming more and more critical. The demands of the Japanese government were treated with contempt. Finally three Chinese men-of-war encountered and fired upon three Japanese cruisers. The Japanese retorted by taking one of the ships captive with all on board, running another ashore in a disabled condition, and chasing the third back into Chinese ports badly crippled. War was now on; and for her own sake, as well as for the sake of peace in the East, Japan felt that she must chastise her great ancient foe. She enlisted to fight for the independence of Corea, for the enlightenment of China, and for the honor of her own name.

CHAPTER XXI.

CONFLICT AND VICTORY.

MATSUDA returned home one sultry afternoon meditating deeply upon the state of affairs that now confronted the country. On every corner he heard enthusiastic discussions as to the probable action of the government, which had not yet officially declared for war. The whole nation was in favor of it, and for years he had felt that it must come sooner or later, for nothing short of conquest would ever open up China to the light of civilization and religion. Whether Japan was prepared for such a campaign was a question to be decided. He dreaded to have his countrymen come into contact with a barbarous power, capable of the unprincipled cruelties that were characteristic of the Chinese. One good result was noticeable already. The opposing parties at home had now forgotten their partisan strifes, and had united as one mass in proclaiming their devotion to their country. Opposition to foreigners had ceased, and all respect was shown to the citizens of American and European countries, whence they had learned the arts of peace as well as of warfare.

Matsuda had just finished drinking a cup of tea when a letter was handed to him from Shiro, who was still attending the Doshisha University at Kioto. Before returning for his summer vacation he had gone with a party on the new railroad down to Osaka, and wrote to his parents about the wonderful sights he saw there. A paragraph in this letter caused the fond father to have greater confidence in the strength of the government, as well as in the sagacity of his son. It was as follows:

"After visiting the great manufacturing industries of the metropolis, and passing through the grounds of the ancient royal castle, we were next allowed to go through the arsenal. It is true that I have never seen much of the world, and have but little practical knowledge of it, but after being here I am convinced that Japan has a force of artillery unsurpassed in almost any country. There we saw rows and rows of great guns just like those brother used to tell about in America. In fact, some were reduplications of the great German guns that created such a sensation at the World's Fair in Chicago. These guns were not imported, but made on the spot by our own craftsmen, and managed entirely by Japanese officers. There was not a foreigner connected with the whole establishment. Some idea of the strength and capacity of these guns may be derived from the statement of one of the officers, who told me that the whole cost of firing one of the largest was about $750. I dread to see such destructive weapons used against even our foes, yet if that be the only way to preserve order and advance national progress, I am in for the contest with all my heart. We have a righteous cause, and I believe God will help us out."

"A chip from the old block," said Matsuda, with a smile, as he folded up the long sheet and laid it in a little drawer.

"I believe Shiro has the right conception, and I shall not give myself further uneasiness as to the probabilities or results of the war."

"But," said Jeannette, "suppose they should need more soldiers and should ——"

She stopped and glanced hesitatingly at Jiro, who was sitting on the other side reading the evening paper. Dropping his paper and looking up quickly he exclaimed,

"I would be the first to enlist!"

"And leave me?" asked his wife reprovingly.

"I pray your lofty pardon if I shocked you," replied Jiro with his old-time courtesy. "You may rest assured that my preference is always to be at your side, but when my country calls I must go. My ancestors died for her, and I would willingly follow their example. Not being a native of Dai Nippon it is hard for you to understand the self-sacrificing spirit that is in every patriotic citizen."

"That is my brave son," said his mother, looking on him with an expression of maternal pride. "Your father is now past the meridian of life and can not be so active as formerly in his country's service. I am grateful that I have sons who can take his place. Be of good courage, my daughter, he has not yet been called upon, and may not be; yet if he must go we can follow him with our prayers, and I believe God will preserve him and the cause for which he fights."

Jiro smiled at this pious remark, but had too much respect for his parents and wife to say what he thought. Besides, he was not so much opposed to Christianity now, and often sat quietly in the room during family worship. His respect was unconsciously growing. As it was now time for him to attend a club meeting he took his leave, and the conversation dropped for a time.

CONFLICT AND VICTORY. 183

Day by day the excitement increased. News came of a great victory for Japan at the mouth of the Yalu river. Then a fresh call was made for troops to go on a campaign into the interior of China, and Jiro was one of the new recruits. While quartered with a body of troops at Osaka waiting for transportation he wrote a letter to his family, an extract from which might be of interest. He says:

"We expect to sail for China within a few days. There are now quartered here several thousand soldiers. We get somewhat lonesome and impatient, with nothing to occupy us except the daily drills. While we were lounging around a few days ago, trying to shelter ourselves from the heat, Mr. Loomis, a colporteur, visited the barracks, and, contrary to the custom, and to the surprise of everybody, secured permission to enter and distribute Bibles to the soldiers. I suppose the tender recollections of home, and the softening influence of our early departure to the scene of bloodshed, must have unmanned most of us, for within a short while *every soldier in the barracks had received a Bible or Testament.* Some did it merely for the sake of politeness, but nearly all of us were willing to relieve our monotony by reading even the book of Yasu. I read mine with increasing interest, and I assure you that I no longer despise it, for it fills me with awe, and shows me my sins in a frightful way. I now dread myself more than all the weapons of the Chinese, and no one can accuse me of being weak. Several hundred of us have banded together for prayer, and if we perish in battle it will be with petitions upon our lips."

This letter brought unspeakable comfort to the anxious loved ones, for they now felt that Jiro was in the hands of God, who would protect him. In the meanwhile Mr. Loomis, Matsuda and others continued the distribution of Bibles. The Emperor had removed to Hiroshima in order to be nearer the seat of war. There were many troops quartered there, and a Bible was given to each. The commanders freely permitted religious workers to enter the camps, and widespread interest was the result, many being brought to Christ.

Patriotism ran high throughout the land. Every young man aspired to be a soldier so that he might help to fight for his country. Mothers and sisters made many sacrifices to assist in raising contributions to forward the cause. One devout old lady had promised to an idol that she would give $500 of her scanty earnings to build a temple, but when the war came on she besought the idol to let her give the money to help fight for her country. She promised to repay every cent, and stated that if she died before it was paid he might send her to perdition, if only she might help to save the honor of her country.

Cheering news continued to pour in from the field. The Chinese had no patriotism, no loyalty for their Tartar Emperor, and, as a result, their troops threw down their arms and fled before the approach of the victorious Japs. After several reverses, Li Hung Chang, viceroy of China and General-in-chief of the army, was divested of his signs of rank, the yellow jacket and peacock feathers, and was imprisoned, being in danger even of losing his life as an atonement for the defeats that he had suffered. China levied new troops, but they were no more successful than the first. The Japanese continued to march inland and to take port after port. The invading army used

CONFLICT AND VICTORY. 185

well the humane civilization they had learned from the West. No needless suffering was allowed. Prisoners of war were treated so kindly that the natives preferred being captured by the Japanese to being subjected to the barbarities of their own troops. The bitter winter came on, and the besieged hoped that the invaders would have to retire, since they were unaccustomed to the rigors of such a climate. But the Japanese purchased sheepskins and in other ways protected themselves so that they made no halt in the prosecution of the war. China besought England and the United States to plead in her behalf, but they thought it wise not to interfere, only they offered to act as peace-makers if China would make proper concessions to secure peace. Port Arthur and Wei-hai-wei, strategic strongholds, were taken, and then China sent envoys, ostensibly to sue for peace, but it was found that they had no authority to make a treaty and that the wily nation was only seeking to kill time. So the Japanese would not cease fighting until Ambassadors should come who had full authority to act for the government. At last Li Hung Chang was restored to position and sent to Japan on this important business. Japan refused to stop fighting until peace was made, but Li Hung Chang was attacked by a crazy young man and slightly wounded while on his peace commission. The offender was duly seized and all efforts were made to atone for the injury, which led the Emperor to declare an armistice pending further negotiations. On April 15, 1895, peace was formally declared and orders were given for fighting to cease. As conditions of peace China agreed to pay an indemnity of 200,000,000 *taels*,* to grant the independence of Corea, to cede the island of Formosa, and to allow Japan to hold all the territory she had conquered on the main land. Acting, however, upon the "advice" of Russia, who was jealous of such a powerful new neighbor getting a foothold on the Continent, the conquering nation generously gave up the conquered territory of the Liao Tung Peninsula, and only occupied the strongholds temporarily till the indemnity could be paid.

Thus ended one of the most interesting of modern wars. A nation of 40,000,000 conquered a nation of 400,000,000, fulfilling the prediction that "One shall chase a thousand and two shall put ten thousand to flight." Verily a little one has become a strong nation.

The results of the war can be seen in many ways. While bloodshed is always fearful and to be avoided if possible, yet God has made even the wrath of men to praise him. China has been humbled to the dust. She can no longer sneer at foreign improvements. She will be open to Western civilization and to the spread of the Gospel as never before. Corea has also been opened for civilization and Christianity to flow in. In Japan herself the result has been beneficial in a large measure. A new impetus has been given to national life, and new opportunities have been opened for religious work among the soldiers.

---

*A monetary unit of variable value, now worth about $1.33 in United States money.

In spite of the distractions of the war and the absence of so many of the young men, the 625 missionaries in Japan witnessed last year 3,422 converts up to December. The total membership of Protestant churches being now 39,240. There are 364 Protestant churches, 91 of which are self-supporting. Contributions for 1894 amounted to $36,108.86. Presbyterians lead with 72 churches and 11,126 members, Congregationalists next with 70 churches and 11,079 members, Methodists 101 churches with 7,536 members, and Baptists follow with 27 churches and 2,146 members, having entered the field after the others. The Greek Catholic Church reports 22,000 members, and the Roman Catholic Church 49,280 adherents. Neither, however, have this many communicants, but they count all who seem to favor their cause.

At some places officers of the army have arranged for Christian services in Buddhist temples for the benefit of sick and wounded soldiers. Christians have shown themselves loyal, and are thus in greater favor with the government. Not only have the missionaries been allowed to distribute Bibles among the soldiers, but Count Ito, the Premier, has accepted a copy, and announced that the Emperor would also accept one. A handsome volume is now being prepared for his Majesty. We may yet hear great things from it. Japanese Christians are now forming societies for the evangelization of the Chinese, and China may still appropriately call Japan "The Land of the Sunrise," for from Japan is rising China's light of civilization, and the power of the cross of Christ. Wise men long ago predicted that Japan would some day sustain to the continent of Asia the same relation as that of England to Europe. Yezo, the northern island of Japan, is said to have enough coal to supply Great Britain for a thousand years. With all her natural resources, added to her enterprising spirit, the Island Empire is destined to rank among the greatest of earth.

* * * * * *

Jiro returned home much changed by his experiences. He was now truly regenerated, and he lost no time in declaring himself. What he had recently endured had sobered him, and at the same time enthused him with a new purpose. He had never seen gross heathenism before as he had witnessed it in China. He resolved to throw his life into the great work of saving China's millions. Many others conceived of a similar design, and soon they are to begin a campaign for Christ which we hope may be more brilliant and successful than even that of recent fame.

Shiro has at last started to America to college, supported by his older brother. It is a great misfortune that young men should have to go so far to be educated, especially when they could be doing work among their own people while at college if they only had well equipped institutions in their own country. Two hundred young men in the same year attended the University of Berlin, Germany. It is to be hoped that the next generation will have superior advantages at home.

Kiku was recently married to a young native pastor, and a bright future seems before her. Her marriage ceremony was very different from that of her mother many years ago. She was united to her betrothed by the simple and beautiful Christian rite, and her home is one sanctified by Christian associations and Christian work. She has never affected foreign airs, nor assumed foreign dress, in which no Japanese can look at ease, but is as attractive now as ever, and still worthy of her name, Chrysanthemum, the royal flower of the LAND OF THE SUNRISE.

(GOOD BYE.)

www.ingramcontent.com/pod-product-compliance
Lightning Source LLC
Chambersburg PA
CBHW020846160426
43192CB00007B/807